T0248319

THE CURIOUS
BARTENDER
COCKTAILS
AT HOME

THE CURIOUS

BARTENDER

COCKTAILS

AT HOME

More than 75 recipes for classic and iconic drinks

TRISTAN STEPHENSON

Photography by Addie Chinn

RYLAND PETERS & SMALL
LONDON • NEW YORK

ART DIRECTOR Leslie Harrington
EDITORIAL DIRECTOR Julia Charles
HEAD OF PRODUCTION Patricia Harrington
PUBLISHER Cindy Richards

PROP STYLIST Sarianne Pleasant
ILLUSTRATOR Selina Snow
INDEXER Hilary Bird

First published in 2021 by
Ryland Peters & Small
20–21 Jockey's Fields
London WC1R 4BW
and
341 E 116th St
New York NY 10029
www.rylandpeters.com

10 9 8 7 6 5 4

ISBN: 978-1-78879-352-0

A CIP record for this book is available from the
British Library.

US Library of Congress CIP data has been applied
for.

Printed in China

CONTENTS

INTRODUCTION

I enjoy having friends over for dinner, but must confess that I rarely make cocktails for my guests. I think this comes as a surprise to some of them, who (quite rightly) expect someone who has made a living from mixing drinks to be mixing martinis on a nightly basis. There are two reasons why I don't make drinks at home very often: the first is that I drink enough cocktails in my bars as it is, and sometimes it's nice to just crack open a bottle of wine and sit back; the second reason has more worrying implications, as it's for the simple fact that I find mixing drinks at home a bit of a chore. With that little revelation, you might be wondering how this book is going to teach you to become a kitchen cocktail hero, when the person writing the book – the person who has made hundreds of thousands of cocktails over the past two decades – finds it too strenuous a task to shake a cocktail for his own wife.

The problem is that I, like pretty much everyone else on the planet, have never been taught how to make good drinks at home. I was taught to bartend. In a bar. But a professional bar station and a domestic kitchen have very little in common with one another. Asking a top bartender to make world-class drinks at home is no easier than expecting a Michelin star chef to produce a tasting menu from scratch in a domestic kitchen. It's not impossible but it requires a transfer of skill to a different environment, using and sometimes substituting equipment, and doing all of it in what is generally a far more confined space. A change of tack is required, but for a professional bartender it can be a difficult transition to make. To shake off years of training and gained experience and to start all over again with low work tops, no ice-well, and an inefficient arrangement of bins, sinks, and fridges. But for someone who has never worked in a bar, and who has never experienced what it's like to be 'five deep in the weeds' at 11pm on a Saturday night, learning to bartend in a kitchen is not a great challenge at all. And in some respects your kitchen is already fairly well set up for mixing drinks: you have running water, a freezer, plenty of ingredients, and a wealth of utensils. The secret, then, lies in practice and preparation; understanding what you're going to need, when you will need it, and how best to make ready for it. As with cooking, it's entirely possible to produce something delicious and to make an incredible mess at the same time. But unlike cooking, your guests will not be content with seeing a tray laden with beautiful cocktails floating into the room as you kick the door shut and hide a scene of complete devastation in the kitchen. One of the great and curious things about mixing drinks is finding that your friends and family want to witness and comment on the making process. Cocktails are about seeing the motion of the bartender, and witnessing the picking, pouring and stirring of ingredients to a perfect state.

In summary, there are three things that I hope you, dear reader, will take from this book: the first is to understand what equipment and ingredients you need to use or source. Second is to understand the basic techniques you need to master to get the best out of the ingredients, and to look like a pro at the same time. And lastly, I hope you will enjoy learning more about the history of each drink as much as I have, and use this newfound knowledge to expertly choose the ideal cocktail for any occasion.

EQUIPMENT & GLASSWARE

These days there are virtually no limits to the range and variety of bar equipment available to the bartender and home enthusiast. The world's great cocktail bars regularly call for expensive equipment to make their drinks and this builds upon the theatre of the experience, adding value to your evening and validating the cash it costs you. At home, however, a vintage gold-plated cocktail shaker is a luxury that most of us cannot afford and that absolutely none of us need.

So let's set the record straight from the start: you don't need lots of fancy equipment to make great drinks at home. Most of the drinks featured in this book can be produced with nothing more a jigger, a cocktail shaker, a barspoon and a good supply of ice. And even a cocktail shaker can be substituted for a plastic container with a lid or even a jam jar, the barspoon swapped for a dessertspoon, and a sieve/strainer used in place of a bartender's hawthorn strainer. The notion that a cocktail is indulgent and worthy of respect is not something that I think should be challenged, but behind closed kitchen doors nobody cares how elegant the process of making them is. Indeed, as a professional bartender I have travelled the world with little more than a jigger, beaker, barspoon and glass, and still managed to knock together some crowd-pleasing cocktails when the circumstances required me to.

Limes don't have to be squeezed with a fancy lever-style citrus press (often known as a Mexican elbow), and instead of silver ice tongs, any similar tong-type kitchen tool will suffice. When bartending on shift I will, of course, present drinks using the arsenal of tools available to me, but when making a nightcap at home you had best believe that I often utilise some unconventional equipment to achieve common

bartending tasks, and it's not unusual to see me working by the light of the open fridge door. But, for your guidance only, here is a list of the most common bartending equipment and their uses.

JIGGER

The jigger is the most important utensil in the home bartender's arsenal as it allows you to measure ingredients accurately. Doesn't sound like much fun, does it? Perhaps not, but inaccuracy causes imbalance and imbalance is the root of all evil where cocktails are concerned. Get used to thinking about measurements (in millilitres, or in fluid ounces if you must) but more than that, get used to thinking about ratios – 'two parts of this, one part of that'. Where a drink has more than five ingredients this can become tricky, but approaching each drink as a ratio of ingredients rather than a sum of numbers will be useful if you've misplaced your jigger and for when you need double, triple or quadruple quantities. Once you have ratios mastered, you'll find that an egg cup or shot glass can function nicely as a stand-in jigger.

BARSPOON

Probably the second most important piece of kit, a barspoon is basically a weighted teaspoon with a long, usually twisted, shaft. Barspoons are useful for a variety of tasks, the most obvious of which is stirring. Since stirred cocktails require quite a lot of ice, a conventional teaspoon is far too short to reach the bottom of the glass. A dessertspoon or tablespoon is too cumbersome to achieve the required level of gentle manipulation, so that really only leaves you with a barspoon. Except, of course, for the fact that a pair of

chopsticks also does quite a good job of stirring ice in a tall beaker or glass.

Barspoons are however generally quite unreliable when it comes to measuring. The bowl of the spoon varies in volume between brands, but generally sits somewhere between 5 and 10 ml (or the equivalent of 1 and 2 teaspoons). The bigger problem lies in the fact that a 'full' measure from a barspoon varies from person to person and from pour to pour, ranging from a meagre droplet to a wobbly daub of liquid barely held together by a thin meniscus. In my opinion, it's far better to use your jigger for small measures and keep the barspoon for what it's best at, stirring.

There are however a couple of other uses for a barspoon. The ones with a flat, coin-like piece on the end are designed to assist with floating or layering ingredients in cocktails that call for it – Irish Coffee, for example (see page 125). The idea is that you rest the base of the barspoon on the surface of the drink, then pour the ingredient that is to be floated down the spiral shaft of the spoon. The shaft slows the descent of the liquid by twisting it around and the base disperses it evenly over the surface of the drink. The situations that call for such a trick are few and far between however, so I wouldn't go out and buy a spoon for this reason alone. That flat base can also be used in place of a muddler (see page 12) to squash soft fruit or bruise herbs. Beware though – I have seen glasses smashed and hands scarred in the engagement in activities such as these. Do it only as a last resort.

SHAKER

Most shakers are made from stainless steel and are comprised of either a steel 'tin' and 'boston' glass, or of a tin with clip-on strainer and cap known as a 'three-piece' shaker. There are positives and negatives to both designs: the boston tends to hold more liquid and has the benefit of a glass so you have an idea of what you've put in there (and what you haven't). The glass part also means it's breakable and the design means that you need a strainer of some sort to stop the ice from flooding out when you pour the drink. The three-piece is a self-contained unit with a strainer built in, but these shakers tend to suffer from being a bit small – for my appetite, at least.

A large plastic three-piece is surprisingly a good solution, though perhaps not as appealing or good-looking as a stainless steel one, it is virtually unbreakable, easy to clean, and a good insulator of temperature, meaning that your drinks will get colder quicker and with less dilution of flavour.

MIXING BEAKER

This is a large, open-top vessel used for stirring drinks. Any shaker can serve the purpose, but I think it's sometimes nice to stir drinks down in a lipped glass and watch as the corners of the ice cubes round off as the drink chills. If a mixing beaker sounds a lot like a small jug/pitcher to you, you're not wrong at all. The only difference is they tend not to have handles.

STRAINER

Hawthorn strainers are comprised of a perforated metal plate with a coil of wire running around the edge and they sit over the top of the cocktail tin part of a shaker when pouring, so as to hold all the ice back. They are essential if you're shaking cocktails with a boston shaker, but surplus to requirements if it's a three-piece that you have.

Another type of strainer is a julep strainer. These are like large perforated spoons that were originally designed to stop ice from falling in your face when sipping on a Mint Julep (see page 106). They're unsuitable for straining shaken drinks as the holes either get blocked or let too much ice through, but some bartenders like to use them for straining stirred cocktails where there is little risk of tiny ice fragments ending up in the glass.

The final type of strainer, which there's a good chance you have already, is a tea strainer, a.k.a. a small sieve/strainer. Finer (smaller holes) is better where these things are concerned, as tea strainers are used as a secondary strain when pouring some shaken drinks as a means of keeping the fine ice shards produced by aggressive shaking out of your drink. Double straining is a practice that is deemed necessary by many professional bartenders, and there may well be a few occasions at home where a pristine-looking cocktail is called for.

MUDDLER

On occasion it's necessary to get physical with some ingredients and engage in a bit of a scuffle. Whether it's squashing raspberries into submission or ruffling the tips of some mint leaves, extracting flavour from fresh ingredients is sometimes done using a 'muddler'. As stupid a name as it might be, it does exactly as one might expect.

Muddlers are like small police batons and generally made of plastic or wood. If you have a rolling pin in your house, you have no need to buy a muddler (use the money for a nice bottle of bourbon or gin instead) as the bakers' most prized tool will do the job just fine. Note: a muddler is a poor substitute for a rolling pin when flattening pastry dough.

CITRUS JUICER

As I've already mentioned, citrus presses are a useful component of your home cocktail cabinet but are by no means essential. Having said that, lemons and limes are not getting any cheaper, so it's perhaps wise to extract every last drop of juice you possibly can from them!

A lever-style press (referred to by many as a Mexican elbow) is your best bet, and these contraptions do a nice job of liberating the oil from the skin of the citrus fruit too. A standard kitchen citrus reamer will work ok too.

KNIVES AND PEELERS

If you don't have a knife and vegetable peeler in your kitchen drawer already, it raises serious concerns about your commitment to freshly prepared food and drink!

A small vegetable knife (or one of the razor-sharp serrated 'tomato' knives) fits the bill for chopping most fruits, and I opt for one of the 'Y' shaped vegetable peelers for stripping healthy lengths of citrus zest.

ICE PICK

Not the kind you go mountaineering with, but the kind of hand-held pick with one or three spikes on the end that is used to chip away at blocks of ice. This is one tool that can't be substituted easily with another kitchen implement so it's worth investing in one if you're planning on freezing big chunks of ice (which you really should be doing if possible).

GLASSWARE

Your favourite cocktail bar may stock a whole range of seductive glassware finely tuned to meet the needs of different drinks, but truth be told 90% of cocktails can be served in one of three glasses: coupe, highball and old fashioned (also known as rocks).

Settle on a sensible-sized coupe that can handle both a tiny Dry Martini (see page 40) or a shaken higher-volume drink, such as a White Lady (see page 71). The 150-ml/5-oz. size is usually about right – it won't look like a half-full bucket when serving said Martini and it won't be full to the brim when mixing a Cosmopolitan (see page 81). Your highball and old fashioned (rocks) glass will usually be around the same volume, only one will be taller and more narrow and the other more squat, heavier and wider. Think about which drinks you like to make the most and consider which size will suit them. Of course you don't need to limit yourself to only these three glasses – see pages 14–15 for a visual guide to what you might enjoy collecting and using. But remember if the drink tastes good, it tastes good – most often the serviceware is there only to improve the experience and enhance the environment. In my time I have been known to quite contentedly consume cocktails from tea cups, egg cups, or even mixed directly back into the bottle when the need arose!

For chilled cocktails that are served 'straight up' (i.e. no ice), the glasses should always be chilled before use. Serving a cold cocktail in a room-temperature glass is like serving a roast dinner on a cold plate – the hot food cools down a lot quicker, just as a chilled drink will warm up a lot quicker. I personally like to use glasses chilled in the refrigerator for most drinks. These glasses will be at around 1°C, which is an acceptable level above the common temperature range of most drinks (0°C to -5°C). Glasses from the freezer work too (and look cool!), but that freezing cold temperature can be a bit alarming to the lips on the first sip.

You can also chill glasses on the fly by adding a few lumps of ice and some water, then quickly stirring for a minute or so, emptying and pouring in the prepared cocktail. Taking the time to ensure the glass is at the correct temperature is a simple step that makes a big difference – as with most things, preparation is key.

GLASSWARE GUIDE

SHOT

This is a small, straight-sided glass with a solid base; it holds either a single or a double measure and is used to serve shots and shooters. It can also be used as a measure should you lose your cocktail jigger (a common occurrence even for the pros).

OLD FASHIONED (OR ROCKS)

A classic glass that is used for drinks that are served on the rocks (i.e. over ice). It should have a capacity of about 300 ml/10 fl oz. and can also house drinks like whisky and soda.

HIGHBALL

A tall, thin, straight-sided glass used for long cocktails over ice and also for serving spirits with mixers. Anything over 350 ml/12 fl. oz. should suffice.

HEATPROOF (OR LATTE)

Take your pick from the elegant wine-glass-shaped Irish Coffee glass, to the sort of tall, handled glass in which you might get served your café latte.

WINE

Classic small wine glasses are a good all-rounder and can be used for plenty of straight-up or punch-style drinks. Large balloon-shaped red wine glasses can work in place of the popular Spanish-style gin copa/balon glasses.

CHAMPAGNE FLUTE

As there is no real restriction on these, they can be as classic or ornate as you choose, though it a bit of bling is perhaps nice for a celebratory or festive offering.

MARTINI (OR COCKTAIL)

This is a stemmed glass with an inverted cone bowl, mainly used to serve classic cocktails. The term martini glass is often used interchangeably with cocktail glass. The longer the stem, the more ornate. Anything between 150 ml/ 5 fl. oz. and 200 ml/6 fl. oz. should suffice for drinks that are served straight up.

COUPE (OR NICK & NORA)

Also used for classic straight-up cocktails, mini coupes (sometimes known as a Nick & Nora), have a shallow rounded bowl and a speak-easy, jazz-age elegance. A classic coupe has a large, shallow bowl and a longer stem. It can be used as an alternative to the flute for serving Champagne and works well for sparkling cocktails

MARGARITA

This glass is also sometimes called the Marie Antoinette (so named as it is rumoured that the glass was shaped around the curve of her breast...). Note: a martini glass can also be used for a classic, straight-up Margarita.

HURRICANE (OR TULIP)

This multi-purpose glass comes in a number of different shapes and sizes. Generally seen as a glass that holds punches and frozen drinks, like an ice-blended Daiquiri.

TIKI MUG

These are novelty ceramic drinking vessels that originated in Tiki bars for serving Tiki-style, usually rum-based drinks. They depict Polynesian or tropical themes, the most common being the Easter Island Moai statues. Despite being called mugs, they don't have a handle.

TANKARD

Often made from hammered copper, these handled cups are classically used to serve the Moscow Mule cocktail. Also, a traditional 'Purl' tankard (made from pewter or stainless steel) is used to serve the earliest known hot alcoholic beverages, like the Flip, where traditionally a hot poker was plunged into the liquid to heat it.

KITCHEN INGREDIENTS

Unless you're content drinking cocktails made entirely from booze (which can be very nice sometimes), you will need a basic catalogue of kitchen ingredients. There's a good chance you're holding stock of this stuff already, but it's worth taking the time to check before embarking upon an evening's cocktail making.

SALT

Perhaps not an obvious cocktail ingredient, but salt performs a similar role in mixed drinks as it does in food: elevating flavour and softening bitterness, sweetness and acidity. Cocktails rarely taste salty, but a small pinch of salt will improve most drinks – you'll see I use it in both the Lime Rickey and Piña Colada recipes. Keep table salt for making syrups and infusions, and flaked sea salt for rimming glassware (as in a Margarita) and garnishing.

SUGAR

Caster/superfine sugar is a staple product that can easily be converted into a simple syrup for cocktails, or used as a base for flavoured syrups. You may wish to experiment with darker sugars too, such as Demerara and muscovado – these work particularly well in cocktails that call for aged rum. Make up a batch and have it to hand for when any recipe calls for Sugar Syrup. For Brown Sugar Syrup , simply follow the recipe below substituting brown sugar for white.

To make 1 litre/1 quart of simple sugar syrup mix 600 g/3 cups of sugar with 400 ml/1¾ cups cold water and heat gently in a saucepan until all of the sugar is dissolved and the liquid becomes clear. Store in the fridge – any clean strewtop jar, like a large jam/jelly jar is an ideal container.

HONEY

A great modifier that can be used in place of sugar syrup in almost any cocktail, assuming you like the flavour of honey of course. Honey plays especially well with grain-based spirits like gin, vodka and whisky.

MAPLE SYRUP

Similarly to honey, maple syrup adds a buttery, candied note to mixed drinks, and it works rather well with American whiskey.

AGAVE NECTAR

Disproven as a health food it might be – but you're not drinking Margaritas because they're healthy, right? – agave nectar certainly has a strong affinity with agave spirits (tequila, mescal) as well as cachaça and agricole rums.

CITRUS

Citrus fruits store reasonably well and provide both theatrical and aromatic effect when freshly squeezed into a drink. Lime is generally the sourest of the family and can be as sour as 1.8 pH. Lime is comprised of both citric and ascorbic acid, whereas lemon is almost entirely citric acid and around 2.3 pH. Orange and grapefruit have a similar pH to one another of around 3.7 (oranges have more sugar in them, so taste less sour).

HERBS

Fresh herbs can be used as visually attractive and aromatically pleasing garnishes as well as components of the cocktail itself. Fresh herbs can be tricky to store however. Too much moisture can make the leaves go slimy and too little moisture makes them dry out, while excessive light turns them yellow. Store soft herbs like mint, basil and coriander/cilantro in the fridge, but arrange them like a bunch of flowers in a glass jar with water in the bottom. Woody herbs, like rosemary, thyme and sage, should also be refrigerated, but last longer when wrapped in damp kitchen towel and placed in a sealable container.

SPICES

Warm cocktails enjoyed in the winter months, benefit from dried spices. If you plan to mix up hot toddies or festive drinks, you might want to rummage and see if you need to replenish storecupboard stocks of any of the following: nutmeg (always best freshly grated), cinnamon (ground and sticks), cloves and star anise. Peppercorns, both black and pink, can be useful too.

EGGS

The use of eggs, egg yolks and egg whites in cocktails has a long history. Many old-fashioned drinks like flips, possets and syllabubs require a whole egg for both a flavour and textural addition to a drink. Lots of cocktails that emerged from the golden era of mixed drinks (1860–1930) also call for egg white in the drink, such as the White Lady or Clover Club. Note: Eggs should be free-range and very fresh, and always wash your hands after cracking egg shells and before touching any other ingredients or equipment.

PICKLES AND PRESERVES

If you are fixing cocktails often, it makes sense to keep a jar of good Maraschino cocktail cherries on hand (but not the day-glow glacé kind used for baking). They are an essential garnish for a Manhattan – look out for the Luxardo brand. Also, a jar of small, green brined olives, stuffed or otherwise, for your Martini, and a jar of cornichons might also come in handy. All can be stored in the fridge. Oh and marmelade, if the Breakfast Martini on page 44 grabs your attention!

SODAS AND MIXERS

It may sound simple, but keeping a good stock of sodas and carbonated mixers can be a bit of a challenge as they tend to lose their fizz quite quickly once opened.

A G&T without the bubbles is a sorry affair, just as a Mojito without that lick of spritz can also feel a bit flat. Soda water, tonic water, ginger beer and cola should make up the four pillars of your carbonated world and should always be freshly opened and well chilled.

A WORD ABOUT ICE

Last, but far from least... let's talk about ice...

The simplest mistake when setting up a home bar is not having enough ice. As a rule, you're going to need about twice as much ice as you think you will. Cocktails get through lots of ice and too little ice in the preparation or service of a drink will always result in an inferior looking and tasting drink. Try to reserve a drawer in your freezer purely for ice, so you can store ice cubes and larger lengths, even blocks of ice that can be chipped away at if the feeling takes you.

It's cubed ice that will be the bread and butter of your drink-making regime however, so invest in some large ice-cube trays and get used to freezing, dumping and refilling them when you have a spare moment. You may wish to purchase a hand-operated ice-crusher – these items are inexpensive and produce good-quality ice nuggets that can be used for a variety of (usually) rum-based cocktails. A dish towel and a mallet can work as a last resort, but it can be tricky to achieve a consistent quality with this method. Blenders cannot be used to make crushed ice – they make snow.

The shape and size of the ice used makes little difference to the final temperature and dilution of a drink. Crushed, cubed and even big rocks of hand-cracked ice of the same weight all eventually achieve about the same levels of dilution and temperature. Only the time this takes changes because the surface areas of the different ice types vary. Stirring with crushed ice might take a Martini down to -5°C in ten seconds but stirring the same Martini with the same weight of hand-cracked ice can take over two minutes to achieve the same levels of temperature and dilution.

The golden rule, no matter what type of ice you use, is to always take it straight from the freezer. Ice from the freezer is colder, of course, but crucially it is not 'wet' (partially melted) and therefore not going to unnecessarily dilute your drink.

THE SCIENCE OF FLAVOUR

There's a lot going on when you take a sip of any cocktail. Tongue, mouth, nose, eyes and even ears work in harmony to glean every ounce of relevant information about the drink you're sipping. In fact, flavour is amongst the most complex perceptions created by our brains.

Let us first see a description of how flavour is produced by flavour psychologist Jean Anthelme Brillat-Savarin in 1825:

> *Man's apparatus of the sense of taste has been brought to a state of rare perfection; and, to convince ourselves thoroughly, let us watch it at work.*
> *As soon as an edible body has been put into the mouth, it is seized upon, gases, moisture, and all, without possibility of retreat. Lips stop whatever might try to escape; the teeth bite and break it; saliva drenches it: the tongue mashes and churns it; a breathlike sucking pushes it toward the gullet; the tongue lifts up to make it slide and slip; the sense of smell appreciates it as it passes the nasal channel, and it is pulled down into the stomach… without… a single atom or drop or particle having been missed by the powers of appreciation of the taste sense.*

Brillat-Savarin, *Physiologie du Goût*
(The Physiology of Taste), 1825

It is fairly common knowledge that as much as 80% of flavour is recognised as a result of the nose, rather than the mouth. This is mostly true, though it's difficult to quantify exactly how much work the nose does in comparison to all the multi-sensory (or multimodal) inputs that the brain utilises. The brain's ability to combine taste, touch and smell into a unified flavour image is called synesthesia.

SMELL

Much of this 'flavour-mapping' work is conducted through retro-nasal smell, that is 'backward' smell, through the back of the nose.

As we gargle, masticate, swill and swallow, tiny aromatic molecules, only visible on an atomic level, are exhaled up through the throat and out of the nose. As they pass through the nasal passage, they come into contact with the olfactory epithelium – this nasal tissue is the nose's direct hard-line to the brain. It sends minute signals to the olfactory bulb, which converts signals into a smell image, the main component of flavour. Contrary to whatever bad publicity you may have heard about the human sense of smell, it is truly an incredible thing – better, in fact, than even the most advanced molecule-detecting equipment that our brains have been able to devise.

TASTE

Taste and the palate also play an important role in flavour perception. Taste begins with the taste buds – a collection of sensory cells, each with fine hairs that respond to stimuli. Taste buds are located within the tiny visible folds on the surface of the tongue, known as papillae. The different receptors in taste cells detect five primary tastes: salt, sweet, sour, bitter and umami (a savoury-like taste which is particularly common in tomatoes, soya/soy and Parmesan cheese). These tastes are detected all over the tongue, though some areas have higher concentrations of specific receptors. Signals are sent to the brain for processing, along with other sensory input.

The tongue and mouth also conduct the important role of detecting mouth-feel. Although more relevant to eating than drinking, mouth-feel can have a profound effect on our appreciation of cocktails. Mouth-feel is not a wholly understood science, but it is known to include such sensory submodalities as touch, pressure, temperature and pain. Each of these affects the image of flavour in different ways. Ever noticed how flat cola tastes different to fizzy cola? That'll be the pain receptors in your mouth altering the flavour image when triggered by the tickling of CO_2 gas in the bubbles of your coke.

VISION

In the most basic form, our eyes tell us whether something will fit into our mouths, and whether or not it's likely to hurt us. But going deeper, the way that a drink looks plays a huge part in how we determine its flavour. I'm not just talking about pretty garnishes (although they do help), but fundamental things such as colour, size, glassware and temperature indication (frosted, steam).

My favourite experiment, which I have conducted on several occasions, is feeding someone blue tomato juice (made by agar clarification and blue food colouring). Even though the taste and aroma have not been altered at all, most subjects fail to recognise the drink as tomato juice, simply because the colour has no relevance to the fruit. Once a lady that I gave blue tomato juice to told me that it tasted like laundry fluid – clearly she was heavily influenced by the bright blue colour.

SOUND

Even sound has an important part to play in the discovery of flavour. The French playwright Molière described the sound of wine as 'glouglou':

How sweet from you
My bottle true;
How sweet from you
Your little glouglou

Act 1, Scene 5, *The Doctor in Spite of Himself*, 1666

And it is true that red wine has an entirely unique sound over other liquids. The glouglou sound of wine as we swallow is the muscle activity in our throats processing red wine's unique texture.

OTHER FACTORS

There is a huge variety of other factors that are thought to contribute towards the 'flavour map' of a drink – even our sense of well-being, comfort and the environment around us affect flavour. Hot soup is better when you're cold and a chilled glass of Sauvignon Blanc tastes better when you're hot. Likewise, continental beers never taste as good as when sipped on a hot sandy beach in their country of origin. A dish from childhood, such as your mother's shepherds' pie or meatloaf, will always taste better (or worse) than any other, since it evokes a sense of nostalgia.

The human appreciation of flavour is a marvellous thing, and something that should be exercised, enjoyed and tested wherever possible. The complex neural pathways that process the data input from our senses all converge in a part of the brain called the primate neocortex. Here we experience a conscious flavour perception, something that is tangible within our minds. And perhaps the smartest trick of all is that of the brain reflecting the data back down to the tongue and fooling us into thinking the whole experience took place in our mouth!

SUGAR Sugar is pure energy. As humans we love the stuff – hell, you can add sugar to almost anything and we'll probably enjoy it more. There is a primal desire for sugar programmed into every one of us right from birth. Sugar does have the effect of slightly reducing the perception of alcohol in a drink. Exactly why this is the case is not clear, though it might be partly due to sugar reducing the volatility of the alcohol (how readily it will evaporate). It could also be a result of the brain's 'reward' system, wherein the effect of the alcohol is lessened as a result of the positive sweet trigger. Our reward system recognises the calories present in the sugar and chooses to ignore the negative chemesthesis effects (see Alcohol, opposite page) of the alcohol. Liqueurs are the perfect case in point. Think about how a 40% ABV liqueur slips down a lot easier than 40% straight vodka.

Tests have shown that sugar suppresses the intensity of bitter, acidic and salty flavours, too. But it does more than that: it actually makes those other tastes more pleasurable than if they were stand-alone – the satisfaction of a bitter-sweet glass of ale, the refreshing acid sting of a kiwi fruit, the indulgence of salted caramel.

BITTERNESS Bitterness is by far the most complicated of the taste senses. It is thought that the tongue detects over 100 different types of bitterness (though salt is just salt).

Unlike sugar, we are programmed with an aversion to bitterness. It's thought that this is as a result of most bitter substances being poisonous in sufficient quantities. (The flip side of this is that in smaller quantities bitter ingredients are often medicinal – think of the anaesthetic effect of chewing on a clove and the antimalarial properties of quinine. Remember your first cup of black coffee? Or your first lager? Chances are that it didn't go down all that well! Bitterness on its own is not nice, and it would require a huge amount of sensory training to convince your brain otherwise. But we're not going to give in that easily! Bitterness has a strange drying effect on the tongue that makes you want to refresh your palate. When we drink something intensely bitter, it's almost like an instant thirst inducer,

COCKTAIL TASTE SCIENCE

Looking at the last 200 years of cocktail evolution, we have seen some clues as to why we have landed upon such an eclectic selection of drinks. Many of the advances in cocktail preparation give key indicators as to why we prefer to enjoy drinks one way more than another, and it's this knowledge that has laid the path for cocktail creators over the years.

We can now go a step further, into the component tastes of a cocktail, and see both how they affect our sense of perception and how they affect each other in the context of a cocktail. Primary taste sensations of saltiness or sweetness are well known to us, but what is not as fully understood is the complex relationships that these tastes have with each other and how they play a role in balancing drinks.

meaning that another sip is required. And another. So when bitterness is accompanied by aromatics and sweetness (and salt), it can become incredibly addictive! The best example of this is the classic gin and tonic – surely one of the greatest refreshments the world has ever known.

Adding bitters to mixed drinks helps us to engineer a more interesting and complex cocktail by fusing together intense bitterness with other taste and aromatic stimuli.

ACIDITY When we eat or drink something intensely sour, we screw our faces up and wince in the wake of it. Intense sourness is experienced negatively, since its consumption generally has no nutritional benefits – so why waste energy eating it?

On the plus side, however, acidity does an excellent job of balancing other taste sensations. Without sourness, ripe fruit is simply sweet; even the accompanying aromatics in a fresh peach fail to deliver that heady feeling of gustatory perfection, since there is no acid either to balance the sweetness or to grip the palate.

In cocktails we often use sourness, balanced with sweetness, to emulate the taste of ripe fruit. Limes and lemons are mostly used, since they have a relatively neutral flavour profile dominated almost entirely by their sourness.

SALT According to Hervé This's 2006 book, *Molecular Gastronomy*:

> '[Salts] selectively suppress bitterness (and probably other disagreeable tastes as well) while intensifying agreeable tastes.'

In my experience, a small addition of salt almost always improves the taste of a cocktail, cordial, liqueur or syrup. The one major exception being if the product is already noticeably salty – through the use of a salty ingredient, perhaps. It is curious, then, that it is such an under-utilised ingredient in cocktails. A great example of where it is used is in the Gin Rickey. This drink is basically a Gin Fizz, or Tom Collins, but with lime juice substituted for lemon juice. Yet in some cultures, most notably India, the sugar is omitted and a small amount

of salt is used in its place. What, on paper, would appear be a very sour drink actually becomes softer and really very tasty. Salt is a much more common beverage ingredient in hot climates, since in the right quantities it is thought to aid in maintaining adequate hydration. Salt lowers perception of sourness significantly, but only slightly affects the intensity of bitter or sweet things.

UMAMI The discovery of the fifth taste, umami, seems like a new thing, but it was actually over 100 years ago, in 1908, that Kikunae Ikeda at the Tokyo Imperial University established its existence. Not salty, sweet, sour or bitter, umami produces a strange sensation that can best be described as savoury. Umami is not a taste that crops up all that often in cocktails. Sure, tomato juice-based drinks like the Bloody Mary have their fair share of savoury kick, but it pretty much ends there. Given the strong savoury connotations of umami it's not all that surprising that bartenders use very little, since one of the main functions of a cocktail is to whet the appetite, not suppress it...

ALCOHOL Almost all spirits have some flavour, even the vodkas. This may come from residual fusel oils or higher alcohols remaining from the distillation process, or traces of the product that the spirit is made from. In the case of vodka, this might be a slight cereal note, or a buttery potato flavour.

Pure ethanol (alcohol) is almost completely flavourless. However, when mixed with water at certain specific concentrations, it does have a slightly bitter-sweet taste. In addition to this, ethanol and acetone (a flavourful ketone) both have a dehydrating effect on the palate, which in turn gives a sense of astringency. Chemesthesis is a term meaning the feel or sensibility of a chemical – ethanol in this case – on the skin, taste buds, mucous membranes, throat and stomach. Alcohol plays havoc with certain nerve channels and the result is the perception of burning. It just so happens that the same nerves triggered by alcohol are the ones triggered by capsaicin (the stuff that makes chillies hot). While pain isn't a taste *per se*, it does have a knock-on effect on our perception of tastes and aromas.

THIRTEEN BOTTLES

All ingredients are equal, but some are more equal than others. While it's true that some cocktails require highly specific brands or styles, most of the time the exact product that you choose to use won't be of critical importance. It's a common understanding that a cocktail is only as strong as its weakest link, but in reality not all links in the chain are of equal size.

If you're making a Martini, the gin is an important consideration as it is at the forefront of the flavour profile, so a little more care in selection is required. In a cocktail such as the Negroni, where the gin battles against far more powerful flavours than that of the dry vermouth in the Martini, there is clearly less need to be fastidious about the brand of gin. In fact unless you're using a gin with wildly extreme botanicals, or one that tastes bad, in all likelihood your Negroni will taste good made with most brands of gin.

I liken it (like a lot of things) to cooking. If you're making *spaghetti alla bolognese*, the exact cut of minced/ground beef is not as important as the tomatoes, cooking time, quality of the pasta etc. If you're frying a steak, however, the cut of beef becomes a very important factor. Which is more important in a Bloody Mary – the brand of vodka or the quality of the tomato juice?

What I'm trying to say here is that in most cases it's ok to select a single brand from each of the main spirit categories (gin, vodka, whisky, rum, tequila, cognac) and stick with it for the majority of your cocktail making. This practice will save you a lot of space and expense and ensure that your spirit cupboard doesn't contain a bunch of dusty neglected bottles.

My main piece of advice is that you make sure you pick one that is versatile, of a premium quality and pleasing to drink neat. For most drinks a generic spirit from the given category will do, but in some instances certain cocktails call for quite specific spirits (you just can't put a Navy rum in a Mojito, for example), so I will do my best to point out any drinks where I believe that a specific style, age or brand of liquor is required.

GIN

More classic cocktails have gin as their base than any other spirit. Indeed, if you were a bartender practising your trade in the 1920s, the vast majority of the drinks you would be asked for would contain gin. For me, gin is all about juniper, so opt for a classic style such as Beefeater or Tanqueray. There are, of course, many newer brands that will also fit the bill.

RUM

A spirit derived from sugar cane, rum is a key component to many classic punch drinks, most notably those from Cuba and drinks that fall under the category of tiki. It's difficult to buy a one-size-fits-all bottle of rum, as some drinks call for lighter styles (un-aged or lightly aged) typical of the Spanish-speaking islands and others for much heavier styles that you might find in Jamaica or Guyana. A good compromise is a light Barbados or St. Lucia rum, such as Doorly's or Chairman's Reserve.

BOURBON

American whiskey is a staple ingredient of many a pre-Prohibition cocktail. Drinks of that era also used rye whiskey as a base, which takes on a slightly spicier flavour when compared to the slick sweetness of

bourbon's higher corn content. A good compromise is Woodford Reserve or Bulleit, both of them bourbons that contain a healthy measure of rye in the mash bills.

SCOTCH

A decent blended Scotch is what we're after here and it needn't break the bank. Avoid anything too smoky as this may imbalance the cocktail, and look for fruit and malt characteristics. Johnnie Walker Gold Label Reserve, Dewars 12 or Chivas Regal 12 will all do the job fine.

COGNAC

French brandy was the original mixing spirit in the mid-19th century, and it remains a fantastically versatile cocktail ingredient (and one that is unrecognised as a cocktail base). A good VSOP from any of the major Cognac houses will work perfectly well here, though if you want my recommendation I would suggest looking at Pierre Ferrand.

TEQUILA

The golden rule when buying tequila is only buy a bottle that says 100% agave on the label. If it doesn't say this, it means the spirit contains some corn- or wheat-based distillate, which serves to boost the alcohol content and dilute the natural vegetal flavours of the plant upon which the drink should be based. Aged tequila can taste quite different to the unaged stuff, so to cover all bases I suggest using a *reposado* ('rested') tequila which will have been aged for between 2 and 12 months.

VODKA

Let's not sugarcoat it – nine times out of ten it's difficult to discern the difference in a vodka once it's been mixed into a cocktail. That one time however, such as when you mix a Vodka Martini, will demand a decent liquid so it's worth buying something you'd be happy to sip on. My recommendation is for a rye vodka like Belvedere or Vestal, or a potato vodka like Chase.

TRIPLE SEC

Triple sec (meaning extra dry in French) is similar to curaçao which has its origins in the Dutch island of the same name. Both are orange liqueurs made from the peels of bitter oranges, but curaçao tends to be sweeter. I would recommend a triple sec such as Cointreau and the recipes I provide are based on a spirit of that sweetness.

MARASCHINO

This cherry-flavoured liqueur is arguably just as important as triple sec in the field of cocktail modification. It came into popularity around the same time as its orange counterpart too. Maraschino has miraculous mixing powers, and the ability to pull a poor-tasting drink out of a nose dive just from a splash. Luxardo is the go-to brand here.

AMARI

Bitter aperitivo like Campari or Aperol are fantastic ingredients to keep around because they make delicious long cocktails like the Americano, as well as being the chief component of the legendary Negroni cocktail.

VERMOUTH

If you're looking for a one-bottle solution to vermouth, I suggest plumping for a bianco style, which is light in colour but still rather sweet.

If your budget can stretch to two bottles, get one extra-dry (French style) and one sweet (a.k.a rosso, Italian style). Always store your vermouth in the fridge and aim to finish the bottle within 30 days (tip: you can always mix it with soda and ice for a delicious alternative to a white wine spritzer).

DRY AMONTILLADO SHERRY

Yes, I am a bit of a sherry fiend, but it's also my belief that a small drop of sherry will have the effect of improving virtually any cocktail it comes into contact with. It often works well in place of vermouth too, and there are great classic cocktails such as the Sherry Cobbler that rely on sherry as the base ingredient.

ABSINTHE

Contrary to what you might have heard (or perhaps experienced), absinthe is not the hallucination-inducing poison that it is sometimes portrayed as. It is typically quite high in alcohol (this is to stop the liquid from looking cloudy as it contains oils that fall out of solution in low-alcohol conditions), but it is not designed to be consumed this way. Absinthe is best imbibed with plenty of ice-cold water, or as an ingredient in such classic cocktails as Sazerac and Corpse Reviver No. 2. The best brands are those produced by Jade, as well as Butterfly and La Clandestine.

MAKING A DRINK

It might seem like a no-brainer to stress the importance of how you shake, stir and use ice (see page 18). But it's easy to overlook the complexity of these techniques and in doing so, overlook some crucial variables that can be manipulated to your advantage. Both the temperature and the degree of dilution of a cocktail are key contributors to the enjoyment of the cocktail, so insuring they are managed correctly is a hugely important part of bar craft.

The common belief is that colder drinks taste better. As temperature lowers, the drink becomes more viscous, texture becomes thicker and more pleasant. Alcohol evaporation is suppressed so that the initial hit of liquor feels softer and increases gently as the drink warms on the tongue. Low temperature also provides a greater feeling of refreshment and cleansing to the palate. Very cold drinks also have less aroma. Vapour pressure is a term that describes how readily a liquid vaporises, and it's the liquid's vapour that we smell when we stick our noses into a glass of wine.

Vapour pressure lowers as temperature lowers, meaning that colder drinks have less aroma. This has an interesting effect when we come to drink a cocktail, as when the liquid quickly heats up in your mouth it begins to pump increasingly intense waves of aroma down your throat and back out through your nose as you breathe.

Good chilling goes hand in hand with ice meltage. Many bartenders have created elaborate routines to limit dilution, but the truth is that a bit of dilution in a drink can actually be a positive thing. But when does not enough dilution become too much? Looking at different bottles of gin, you can see from the wide variety of bottle strengths that producers are careful to package the product at exactly the right ABV to best show off the flavour. The same is true for cocktails – the ABV of a finished drink will affect both the taste of the drink and the aroma, where a little extra water can persuade a greater number of aromatic molecules to escape the glass (which is why water is often added to whisky).

Most of the time dilution is a subjective science, but I have found that sometimes the amount of water in a cocktail is of critical importance and can easily ruin a drink when insufficient care is taken. The key is understanding how and why chilling and dilution occur, then adjusting our techniques to achieve the results we're after – just as a chef adjusts cooking time to meet the needs of each individual dish.

SHAKING

Shaking a cocktail chills it quickly. This is in part because the agitation of the ice and liquid speeds up the process of equilibrium, but also because the ice cracks and breaks, increasing its surface area. Shaking a drink for more than ten seconds will have very little further affect on temperature or dilution. This is because as the cocktail approaches its freezing point, its temperature plateaus. At this point the level of dilution will also plateau, since the ice is only required to stabilise the temperature of the drink (against the warm air outside of the shaker), rather than chill it.

Shaken drinks are also 'aerated' to a degree – the action of whipping up the cocktail with ice causes air bubbles to become trapped in the liquid for a time. We are able to detect these tiny bubbles on the palate, and they can profoundly affect the tactile experience of the cocktail and the way in which flavour is perceived.

The vibrant Japanese bar scene has contributed a number of great things to western bartending over the past few years. A significant influence that has come out of Japan has made a lot of western bartenders reconsider the way in which they shake. When I first heard about the 'Japanese hard shake' I assumed it was a way of shaking a drink hard, but if anything it should refer to how hard it is to master. The aim is to bounce the ice off every surface of the shaker by moving the shaker in a highly specific pattern. The intended result is a drink that, quite simply, feels better. The pioneer of the technique, Uyeda San of Tender Bar in Tokyo, is adamant that the drink is better in every way, but in tests I have discovered that the pattern in which you shake (as long as it's not excessively slow) makes no difference to the temperature or dilution of the cocktail – once again science wins over. That leaves only the element of aeration. Sadly, measuring aeration and viscosity is much harder to do and requires in-depth qualitative testing to be able to truly determine whether the hard shake really does make a better drink.

Be sure to use plenty of ice in the shaker – fill it two-thirds full for a single drink and add extra ice if you're shaking a lot of liquid. Clip the lid or tin on to the shaker and give it a fast and hard shake for five to ten seconds.

STIRRING

A strong drink can be chilled to -3°C in under ten seconds by shaking it with cubed ice, but to achieve the same result by stirring with cubed ice will take over 30 seconds. This is because a stir is, in a sense, a very slow shake. You can be forgiven for assuming that a stirred drink has more dilution because it takes longer, but the physics are the same whether the drink is shaken or stirred – if a cocktail is stirred for long enough, it will reach almost exactly the same temperature and dilution as if it were shaken. I say almost, because the longer exposure to the warm air surrounding the beaker will create some extra dilution in the drink.

The most important thing to understand about stirring is that it takes rather a long time – more than a minute in many cases if you're aiming for really low temperatures. Remember that chilling and dilution

plateau in the same way as shaking – after around 120 seconds (depending on the size of the ice) the drink won't get much colder and it won't get much more diluted. You can tell if a cocktail is being stirred well because it's an almost silent process. Ice should not be 'clinking' around (this creates bubbles and chips of ice) but spinning fluidly around the circumference of the beaker or tin. As with shaking, plenty of ice is needed and the level of liquid in the beaker/tin should fall well under the level of ice. Generally speaking, a

one-minute stir should do the trick, but it's fine to go up to two minutes. If you can wait that long for your drink!

BUILDING

There are a lot of cocktails that are quite delicious when simply built over ice in the glass. Besides requiring less equipment and making less mess, there is something rather satisfying about enjoying a drink from the glass that you mix it in. Approach building in the same way as you would approach a stirred drink.

BLENDED

Blenders are becoming a less common sight in modern cocktail bars, but there are still some classics that can only be created in a blender, and other drinks that can benefit from being blended.

In most instances a blended drink will call for the same weight or volume of ice as the volume of liquid ingredients. Blended drinks must be served immediately as they are prone to 'splitting', which is where the slushy ice floats on top of the liquid.

GIN

GIN HAS JOURNEYED FROM BACKSTREET BAR
ROOMS TO THE COCKTAIL LISTS OF THE
MOST EXCLUSIVE HOTELS IN THE WORLD
AND HUNDREDS OF GIN COCKTAILS WERE
MASTERMINDED BETWEEN 1900-1930, NOT
LEAST OF ALL, THE LEGENDARY DRY MARTINI.

AVIATION

50 ML/1⅔ FL. OZ. TANQUERAY GIN
25 ML/¾ FL. OZ. FRESH LEMON JUICE
5 ML/1 TSP MARASCHINO LIQUEUR
5 ML/1 TSP CREME DE VIOLETTE

Shake all the ingredients in a cocktail shaker with cubed ice and fine-strain into
a chilled coupe glass. There's no garnish, but you may choose to perform a salute
to your relevant country of origin.

The first reference I can find for the Aviation cocktail is in the 1916 book *Recipes for Mixed Drinks* by Hugo R. Ensslin. This places the likely creation date of the drink slap-bang in the middle of the golden era of aviation. It's easy to forget, given the mundane commercialization of air travel today, that once upon a time aviators were the rock stars of the world. While the legendary aviator Howard Hughes was still in short trousers, the aviators of the early 19th century were literally armed with nothing more than a pair of flying goggles, a cigarette and a healthy dose of determination, all in the quest for gravity defiance.

Since their conceptions, cocktails have consistently reflected the trends, fashion and icons of their times in both ingredients and titles (the Sidecar, Mary Pickford and Flaming Lamborghini are all examples of this). So it comes as no surprise that a cocktail should be named after the lofty endeavours of the aviator. And not just any cocktail; this one contains gin, traditionally the preferred tipple of flying men, and is even the colour of a morning blue sky. Besides all of that though, it tastes absolutely fantastic in my opinion and ranks highly as one of the best twists on a Sour out there.

When I first tested my mettle behind the stick, the Aviation was commonly recognized to be a Gin Sour with maraschino liqueur in place of sugar. Simple, right? That particular recipe was taken from the classic Harry Craddock's *The Savoy Cocktail Book* (1930). Undoubtedly this is a tasty version of the drink, but it's not the original version, or the best...

To find the original, we must travel back to 1916, and the aforementioned *Recipes for Mixed Drinks* by Ensslin. In this book, we find the original recipe, which has less maraschino than the Savoy version and includes an extra ingredient – crème de violette. This liqueur is flavoured, as the name suggests, with the violet flower. The taste is like that of the little blue candy that you sucked on as a child; floral, sweet and entirely unique. Now this is not a flavour to lead off with – put too much crème de violette in any drink and all you're likely to taste is sickly, grandmother's potpourri, floral assault bomb. Use a couple of dashes like a seasoning, though, and you get a wonderful floral aromatic to accompany the other flavours in the drink, and that's exactly how an Aviation works.

CORPSE REVIVER NO 2

20 ML/⅔ FL. OZ. PLYMOUTH GIN
20 ML/⅔ FL. OZ. TRIPLE SEC
20 ML/⅔ FL. OZ. LILLET BLANC
20 ML/⅔ FL. OZ. LEMON JUICE
2 DASHES ABSINTHE VERT
LEMON ZEST, TO GARNISH (OPTIONAL)

Shake all of the ingredients in a cocktail shaker with plenty of cubed ice then fine-strain into a chilled cocktail glass. You may like to garnish with a strip of lemon zest, but it's not essential, since the drink will all be gone in under a minute. Won't it?

Corpse Revivers were once a whole family of cocktails, dispensed as hangover cures in the morning and as pick-me-ups in the afternoon and early evening. At the beginning of the 20th century it was common for a bar to offer their own proprietary formula for bringing pre-noon patrons back from the brink of death, and these were often listed as Corpse Revivers. Very few of these recipes were ever written down, though, perhaps on account of the questionable effectiveness of the promised revival or the sheer bizarreness of the concoctions, until Harry Craddock listed two in *The Savoy Cocktail Book* in 1930.

But a little digging around tells us that hangover cures have been called Corpse Revivers since at least the early 1860s, some 15 years before Harry Craddock was born. One of the earliest examples I could find features in an 1862 short story entitled *How I Stopped The Brownes From Asking Me To Come To Dinner*, where the narrator visits an American Bar (no, not that one) in London's Piccadilly and is served a Corpse Reviver containing milk and some other unnamed alcoholic ingredients. The drink was thrown between two crystal vessels and, upon drinking it, the narrator remarked that it 'filled [him] with an extraordinary courage and determination'.

Of the two revivers that Craddock penned in *The Savoy Cocktail Book*, the Corpse Reviver No. 2 is the best known and, to be frank, the best (No. 1 is a very different, brandy-based drink). The No. 2 combines gin with triple sec and lemon juice, so were it not for the addition of Lillet Blanc and a slug of absinthe, it would effectively be a White Lady (see page 71). But those two simple modifiers transform the cocktail into something else entirely – the Lillet smoothes over some of the craggy edges of the lemon and orange liqueur, while the absinthe brings herbal zing and adds a kind of ghostly glaucous to the drink's hue.

Craddock commented that 'Four of these taken in swift succession will un-revive the corpse again'. His point being that overdosing on the drink would result in the drinker once again inducing a death-like state.

When four out the five ingredients in your cocktail are alcoholic and three of them are strong spirits, it's wise to approach with caution. With that in mind, I like to make small Corpse Revivers… dainty little things that can be knocked back in a couple of sips like the medicine that they are intended to be.

DRY MARTINI

45 ML/1½ FL. OZ. TANQUERAY TEN GIN
10 ML/⅓ FL. OZ. DOLIN DRY VERMOUTH
LEMON ZEST OR A GREEN OLIVE, TO GARNISH (OPTIONAL)

Add the ingredients to a chilled mixing beaker (from the freezer) and use a barspoon to stir with plenty of cubed ice for at least 90 seconds. Strain into a chilled martini glass or coupe and garnish. This makes quite a small drink. It's far better, in my opinion, to keep things civilized and keep the Martinis cold. It shouldn't take more than 5 minutes to drink it in its entirety, which gives you plenty of time to make another round.

A perfect union of two ingredients in any context – food, drink or otherwise – is a thing worth celebrating. Where the Martini is concerned it would appear that we have achieved just that. The cultural significance of this drink is something that most people are aware of, but the true genius of its making is the preserve of a lucky few. A good Martini is potent, but subtle; complex, but clean; cool, but spicy. Most importantly, perhaps, is the beauty that can be found in its brevity. A Martini cannot (and should not) be savoured if it is to be enjoyed properly. It's an all or nothing affair. Get stuck in quickly, or lose forever that fleeting chill which softens alcohol, crisps up citrus, and consorts to thicken the texture of the drink on the palate.

The history of this drink is a confusing and often contradictory mess. Essentially, the Dry Martini is a riff on the Martini, which first made its appearance in the 1890s. The Martini was itself nearly identical to the Martinez cocktail, the name having likely been changed to indicate the Martini brand of vermouth that was being used to make the cocktail at the time. Cocktail books from the late 19th century seldom list both the Martini and Martinez, which leads many of us to conclude that they were Siamese twins of sorts – different names but put together the same way. The Martinez of 1884 was effectively a gin-based Manhattan consisting of two parts Italian vermouth to one part Old Tom gin, bitters and a splash of sugar syrup. The Martinis that landed during the 1890s were the same, most of them made with sweet vermouth and Old Tom gin.

Other drinks from around that time toyed with the idea of dry gin and French (dry) vermouth. The 'Marguerite', published in 1904 called specifically for Plymouth gin, which was mixed with equal parts French vermouth, orange curaçao and orange bitters. Then there was the Turf Club (first appearing in the 1880s) which opted for sweet vermouth, and Harry Johnson's 'Martine' cocktail, which could have been a misspelling of either Martini or Martinez! The world had to wait until the early 1900s for a Dry Martini recognisable by today's standards; Bill Boothby's *The World's The Drinks and How to Mix them* (1908) calls for equal parts French Vermouth and 'dry English Gin', orange bitters, and to garnish with a squeeze of lemon peel and an olive. There are other references to the drink before Boothby's book, but his is the first I can find that uses French vermouth and dry gin after the modern fashion. Boothby also includes a recipe for a 'Gibson', which is the same drink but without the bitters. Interestingly, we now call a Dry Martini garnished with a silverskin onion a 'Gibson', but Boothby opted for the olive.

Even Boothby's Dry Martini wasn't all that 'dry' when compared with what was to come. The gradual nudging of ratios between gin and vermouth meant that the drink became stronger and less sweet as time went on. As the Martini reached peak dryness in the 1950s – where the slightest glance at a bottle of vermouth, or as Churchill liked to put it, 'a phone-call to France', would suffice – its cold-blooded disposition was the

perfect test of a hard-nosed businessman's resolve. Three-martini lunch, anyone? You bet.

As vodka took over, gin died out, and conservative tastes moved on, too. But far from being ignored, the Martini was brought back to life (kicking and screaming) in the 1980s when any drink served in a Martini glass was called an '*insert flavour here* Martini' – ironically, the only things that tended to be absent from the glass were gin and vermouth!

With cocktail culture now firmly back on track, bartenders have revisited the Martini story and paid homage to this, the holiest of all cocktails. I have spent much time mulling over the multitude of variables that make this seemingly simple drink so frustratingly difficult to get right. The truth is that there's a perfect Martini out there waiting for everyone; the difficulty is fathoming out what's right for you. It's probably for this reason that the Martini has stood the test of time. It's more of a concept than a drink in its own right, primed and ready for customization to each drinker's requirements. Ask a bartender to make you a Martini and you should have at least five questions fired back at

you. Walk away if you don't. Here are but a few of my own observations that I think are worth sharing with you. Take them as you will, as they are not gospel, but merely an insight from someone who, over the years, has imbibed and deliberated over their share of Martinis.

Don't assume that drier is better; for me the sweet spot is somewhere between 3:1 and 6:1 in favour of the gin. Use dry ice cubes (i.e. preferably straight from the freezer), otherwise the drink becomes too diluted and a bit flabby. Do dilute the drink enough; a Martini shouldn't be a chore to get through. Martinis generally need stirring for 90 seconds to reach the best possible temperature, and dilution is a part of that process. It's surprisingly difficult to over-dilute a Martini by stirring too long, so take your time. Shaking is fine if you like it that way and it's certainly a lot quicker. Don't go crazy with the garnish. I think it's debatable whether a Martini needs a garnish at all, but a very small piece of lemon zest or an olive is fine – I've been known to say that it's easier to ruin a Martini with a piece of lemon peel than it is a cocktail shaker.

BRAMBLE

40 ML/1⅓ FL. OZ. TANQUERAY GIN
20 ML/⅔ FL. OZ. FRESH LEMON JUICE
10 ML/⅓ FL. OZ. SUGAR SYRUP (SEE PAGE 17)
15 ML/½ FL. OZ. CREME DE MURE
BLACKBERRIES AND A LEMON SLICE, TO GARNISH

Build the first three ingredients over crushed ice into a chilled rocks glass, then pour
the crème de mure over the top so that it 'bleeds' down through the ice.
Garnish with a few blackberries (or raspberries) and a slice of lemon.

•

For my personal tastes, this recipe is a touch on the sweet side, but it comes straight
from the man himself, so who am I to argue? If you want it a little drier, try taking
5 ml/1 tsp sugar syrup out and adding 5 ml/1 tsp extra lemon juice.

One of the best drinks to emerge from the cocktail car crash that was the 1980s is the Bramble. The drink was invented by legendary London-based liquid guru, Dick Bradsell. At the time, Dick was working in Fred's Club in Soho, a venue that schooled many of the future stars of the London bar scene. Dick based the drink on a Singapore Sling recipe, replacing the Bénédictine and cherry brandy with crème de mure.

But of course it's not. There has to be something special about a cocktail that is so renowned and yet relies on such a simple formula: a gin sour with a dash of blackberry liqueur. Why not strawberry liqueur, or coffee liqueur? Well, I personally think that something special is down to a clever combination of ingredients and a name that ingeniously describes it.

It's simple when you think about it. A bramble is a typically British prickly shrub, just as gin is a traditionally British product. Blackberry is the base of crème de mure, but wild blackberries don't just smell of blackberries, they also take in the smells of all the natural surroundings of the countryside – the earthiness of dried tree bark, the spice of a fallen pine cone or the sweet freshness of wild honeysuckle. These wonderfully nostalgic aromas are present in a lot of gins too: while juniper provides earthiness and pine-like flavours, coriander gives a citrusy spice and angelica introduces the deep, resinous woody notes.

The combination of gin and crème de mure is genius, and couple that with a name that no other word in the English language could better describe, and you have a winning drink.

BREAKFAST MARTINI

50 ML/1⅔ FL. OZ. BEEFEATER 24 GIN
15 ML/½ FL. OZ. COINTREAU
15 ML/½ FL. OZ. FRESH LEMON JUICE
2 TSP ORANGE MARMALADE
ORANGE ZEST, TO GARNISH (OPTIONAL)

Dry shake all the ingredients (i.e. without ice) in a cocktail shaker and give them a good stir with
a barspoon to break up the marmalade. Next add cubed ice, and shake well for 10 seconds.
Double-strain into a chilled martini glass and garnish with a twist of orange zest.

If you ask me, there's nothing wrong with drinking
a regular Dry Martini for breakfast, but I can certainly
see that it might not fit into everyone's morning routine.
Perhaps that's why, in 1996, Salvatore 'The Maestro'
Calabrese developed a slightly more acceptable
companion to a bowl of cornflakes. Salvatore was
running the Library Bar at the Lanesborough Hotel in
London at the time, and I guess there's no better place
to serve a breakfast cocktail than in a posh hotel bar.
The drink was well received, so when Salvatore went
to New York the following year to promote the launch
of his book *Classic Cocktails*, he convinced legendary
bartender Dale DeGroff to let him serve it at New York's
Rainbow Room bar. According to Salvatore, 'Dale
thought [he] was mad using marmalade in a cocktail.'

The drink bears a good deal of resemblance to at
least two classic Savoy drinks that also feature in this
book. First is the Corpse Reviver No. 2 (see page 39),
where the similarly bracing tang of sweet and sour
places the Breakfast Martini firmly in the pick-me-up
category of mixed drinks for the morning after the night
before. Second is the White Lady (see page 71), the
difference here being the lack of egg white and the
inclusion of marmalade, with a slight fiddle with the
ratios to accommodate it. But that's not the only Harry
Craddock drink that this drink is related to. There's
also the Marmalade Cocktail. Originally printed in
Craddock's famous 1930 work The *Savoy Cocktail
Book*, the Marmalade Cocktail was intended to serve six
people. Craddock remarked: 'By its bitter-sweet taste

this cocktail is especially suited to be a luncheon
aperitif.' The cocktail called for '2 Dessertspoonful
[sic] Orange Marmalade, The Juice of 1 big or 2 small
Lemon, 4 Glasses Gin', to be shaken and garnished with
a twist of orange. Personally, I find the Marmalade
Cocktail a little too tart. A glug of sugar syrup soon
sorts the problem out, or the other option is a splash
of triple sec. Of course, by that point you're drinking
a Breakfast Martini...

Salvatore tells me that the inspiration for the drink
didn't come from old drinks books, but from his wife.
Being Italian, Salvatore is not in the habit of eating
breakfast – a shot of espresso usually suffices. But
working late nights takes its toll, and on one occasion
when he emerged from bed looking particularly
haggard, a slice of toast with marmalade was forcefully
shoved into his mouth. 'The bittersweet tang reminded
me of the sweet and sour balance of a good cocktail,'
he says. The rest of the process came easily: gin for
juniper freshness; triple sec to sweeten and to heighten
the orange aromatics, and lemon to balance.

Some will argue that the Breakfast Martini is
a simple twist on a White Lady, or a copy of the
Marmalade. For me it's arbitrary whether Salvatore
adapted the drink or came up with it independently,
because what we know for sure is that very few, if any,
bartenders were making cocktails with marmalade
in 1997. Salvatore changed that, inventing a tasty,
innovative drink that used an ingredient common to
every household and – from then onwards – bar.

BRONX

45 ML/1½ FL. OZ. GORDON'S GIN
10 ML/⅓ FL. OZ. MARTINI ROSSO
10 ML/⅓ FL. OZ. MARTINI EXTRA DRY
25 ML/¾ FL. OZ. FILTERED ORANGE JUICE
A MARASCHINO COCKTAIL CHERRY, TO GARNISH (OPTIONAL)

Shake all of the ingredients in a cocktail shaker with cubed ice and strain into a chilled coupe. (I think this drink is perhaps improved by the use of blood orange juice, or through a combination of grapefruit juice and orange juice.)

Ask a group of bartenders to tell you what the ultimate classic cocktail is, and they will debate long and hard, suggesting such drinks as the Martini, Manhattan, Negroni and Daiquiri. Ask them to tell you which is the worst classic cocktail and they'll come to a decision pretty quickly: the Bronx.

Gin and vermouth is a holy union of ingredients. In virtually any ratio you can imagine, it just works. But throw a measure of orange juice into the mix and suddenly nothing works any more and everything tastes wrong. So why am I including the Bronx in this book? Well, everybody likes an underdog and I like the challenge of attempting to work out what went wrong with this once-popular cocktail and whether there's any way to salvage something delicious from the wreckage.

Like the Bobby Burns, this drink was the product of the long-since-demolished Waldorf-Astoria Hotel on Manhattan Island. It was first mixed in the hotel's Empire Room (the main restaurant) sometime around the turn of the 20th century by bartender Johnnie Solon. This Spanish-American war veteran claimed not to have named the drink after the New York borough, but after the newly opened Bronx Zoo.

When requested by a lunchtime guest to make something 'new', Solon used the Duplex cocktail (equal parts dry and sweet vermouth with orange bitters) as a starting point. Two jiggers of Gordon's gin and a jigger of orange juice were combined with a Duplex. Stars then shot across the noonday sky and African elephants bowed their heads in respect: a new cocktail was born.

As the waiter transported the yellow drink away from the bar, he turned and asked Solon what its name was. Solon remembered that patrons of the Waldorf-Astoria sometimes claimed they saw 'strange animals' after quite a few mixed drinks, which reminded him of his visit to the zoo just two days previously – 'Oh, you can tell him it's a Bronx,' he replied.

Make no mistake about it, this drink was a real hit at the time, especially on warmer days and where a spot of daytime refreshment was in order. And since New York boroughs were obviously a safe naming strategy for cocktails – the Bronx had joined the very popular Manhattan – it likely inspired the creation of the Brooklyn cocktail, too.

As I said earlier, the drink has fallen out of fashion of late. I feel that the contempt directed at the Bronx is not through the fault of the drink, but through a miscommunication of its purpose. At the time of its creation, this cocktail was an antidote to more boozy drinks like the Martini and Manhattan. The Bronx served as a crossover between sours and straight-up spirit-and-vermouth aperitifs. It offers botanical depth, winey top notes and a bite of a fruity acidity to keep you fresh. As a mid-afternoon alternative to Pimm's and lemonade, or a white wine spritzer, the Bronx has the potential to shine (and it's in those situations that I suggest you mix one).

CLOVER CLUB

40 ML/1⅓ FL. OZ. GIN (DARNLEY'S VIEW OR ANY GIN WITH A SPICY KICK)
15 ML/½ FL. OZ. FRESH LEMON JUICE
15 ML/½ FL. OZ. RASPBERRY SYRUP (SEE RECIPE BELOW)
15 ML/½ FL. OZ. MARTINI EXTRA DRY VERMOUTH
15 G/½ OZ. EGG WHITE

Shake all the ingredients in a cocktail shaker with cubed ice then strain into a separate mixing beaker, cover, and shake again with no ice. This 'dry shake' whips air into the cocktail. Strain into a chilled coupe and drink quickly.

Note You can omit the egg white if you prefer, but it adds a lovely sherbet effect to the palate.

FOR THE RASPBERRY SYRUP (MAKES ABOUT 250 ML/1 CUP)

250 G/2 CUPS FRESH RASPBERRIES
A PINCH OF SALT
250 G/1¼ CUPS CASTER/SUPERFINE SUGAR

Toss the raspberries in the salt and sugar. Place in a 1-litre (35-fl. oz.) mason jar, pop it in the fridge overnight and in the morning add 250 ml/1 cup water to the jar. Bring a saucepan of water up to 50°C (122°F) and turn the temperature right down so that it holds there. Pop the mason jar in the water and leave it for 2 hours, giving it the occasional wiggle. When 2 hours are up, carefully remove the jar then strain the contents through a sieve/strainer. To prolong the lifespan of your syrup it's often useful to add a splash of gin or vodka. Store in the fridge for up to 1 month.

Part gin sour, part Martini, part raspberry liqueur, The Clover Club is fruity, dry, delicate and fiendishly addictive. Had it been given half a chance, it could quite possibly have single-handedly saved the 1980s from the depths of drinking depravity. The cocktail was named for and enjoyed by the eponymous Philadelphia-based lawyers' and writers' club founded in 1882. Like many other gentleman's clubs of the time, a signature drink was an essential component of congenial gatherings. The Clover Club drink dates to 1896, as seen in the 1897 book, *The Clover Club of Philadelphia*.

When I first became a bartender, the Clover Club was still dragging itself out of 70 years worth of obscurity. We used to make them with gin, grenadine, lemon and egg white. It was basically a pink gin sour, and even though it tasted nice enough, it wasn't going

to be winning any awards for innovation. The earliest recipe calls for raspberry syrup, not grenadine, and also vermouth. Slowly, we bartenders began to embrace the classic version, and like the unfurling of pink petals the beauty of the true Clover Club blossomed.

And for me it's the addition of a splash a vermouth that really sets the Clover Club apart, where aromatics of thyme and the bitterness of wormwood intercept the raspberry before it becomes overly fruity. That said, the raspberry syrup is probably the most important ingredient. Most off-the-shelf syrups taste more like the devil's confectionery than the concentrated essence of a piece of fresh fruit. Fortunately, raspberry syrup is simple to make at home, so I've included the only recipe you'll ever need above. It's a game changer as far as the Clover Club is concerned.

By Appointment to Her Majesty the Queen
Gin Distillers
Booth's Distilleries Limited London

BOOTH'S
Finest Dry Gin

26·6 FL. OZS. 70° PROOF

Produced in London England
Distilled by Booth's Distilleries Limited
Clerkenwell Road London EC1

HANKY PANKY

40 ML/1⅓ FL. OZ. PLYMOUTH GIN
40 ML/1⅓ FL. OZ. MARTINI ROSSO
5 ML/1 TSP FERNET-BRANCA
ORANGE ZEST, TO FINISH AND GARNISH

Pour all of the ingredients into a mixing beaker and add plenty of cubed ice. Stir for at
least 1 minute, then strain into a chilled martini glass. Twist a small piece of orange zest
over the top to spritz the drink with its oils and drop it into the glass.

I'm not sure there are many people still alive that
throw the outdated phrase 'hanky-panky' into their
normal conversations as a way of describing illicit
sexual relations. But if you were involved in hanky-
panky prior to the 1950s, it's unlikely infact to have
involved any act of a sexual nature. In the late 19th
century, hanky-panky had a broader scope covering
any act that was unethical or underhand.

When the term first came about, in the 1830s, it
was specifically related to paranormal trickery and the
belief in ghosts and apparitions. Perhaps the phrase
came from the much older 'hocus-pocus'. After all,
it does share the same initials, it rhymes, and has a
similar definition. That may also be why 'hanky-panky'
was widely adopted by magicians to describe illusions
and sleight-of-hand trickery.

In 1912, *Hanky Panky* was the title of a short-lived
musical that opened at the Broadway Theatre in New
York. The fact that the phrase had moved into the
lexicon of general entertainers is an important event,
because it is a thespian that we have to thank for the
naming of the Hanky-Panky cocktail.

This occurred around the same time as the stage
musical, but specifics are difficult to come by. What we
do know is that the drink was invented by Ada 'Coley'
Coleman at the Savoy's American Bar in London. Coley
worked at the Savoy from 1903 to 1924, during a period
when women were not permitted to drink in there.

Coleman created the Hanky-Panky for actor Charles
Hawtrey (1858–1923) who, when he wasn't starring in
West End musicals and silent movies, spent a great

deal of time gambling, drinking and getting married/
divorced. Coleman told the story behind the creation
of the Hanky-Panky to *The People* newspaper in 1925:

*The late Charles Hawtrey... was one of the best judges
of cocktails that I knew. Some years ago, when he was
overworking, he used to come into the bar and say, 'Coley,
I am tired. Give me something with a bit of punch in it.' It was
for him that I spent hours experimenting until I had invented
a new cocktail. The next time he came in, I told him I had a
new drink for him. He sipped it, and, draining the glass,
he said, 'By Jove! That is the real hanky-panky!'
And Hanky-Panky it has been called ever since.*

The drink consisted of equal parts dry gin and sweet
vermouth accompanied by a splash of Fernet-Branca
and a twist of orange. The fact that it called for the
more modern dry gin over Old Tom and that it is
essentially a sweet Martini with the addition of Fernet,
suggests that it was conceived in the 1910s, after the
trend for dry gin and dry vermouth in early Martini
cocktails that appeared in the first decade of the 20th
century. The drink shares a great deal of similarity to
Gin & It (equal parts gin and Italian vermouth), which
became very popular in London during Prohibition
(1920–33). It seems likely then that the drink was
created between 1910 and 1920. And since it's unlikely
that Hawtrey was 'overworking' during World War I,
I would place its creation at some point between
1910 and 1914.

FRENCH 75

35 ML/1¼ FL. OZ. G'VINE FLORAISON GIN
10 ML/⅓ FL. OZ. STRAINED FRESH LEMON JUICE
5 ML/1 TSP SUGAR SYRUP (SEE PAGE 17)
CHILLED CHAMPAGNE, TO TOP UP
LEMON ZEST, TO GARNISH (OPTIONAL)

Premix the gin, lemon juice and sugar syrup then pop it in the fridge for 1–2 hours.
This means that no ice is needed, alleviating any dilution of flavour. Once cold, add
this premix to a flute glass and top up with the chilled Champagne.
Garnish with a fine lemon zest twist , if liked.

Sparkling wine is not an easy ingredient to mix with. Be it Champagne, Cava, Prosecco or indeed any other regionally delineated bubbly – these wines tend not to play nicely with others. This is partly down to the simple fact that sparkling wines are designed to be stand-alone ingredients, not intended for jumbling-up with extraneous flavours. It is ironic then, that the other reason that they don't mix well with other ingredients is because they actually don't taste that great in the first place. No need to re-read that last bit... Most people recognise the fact that Champagne isn't especially tasty stuff, but choose to happily push on knocking it back because it's the socially correct thing to do. Wait, you don't like Champagne?! No – not especially. Sure, I'll drink it – because it's wet, contains alcohol, and I get a sadistic kick out of knowing that someone (who isn't me) spent a lot of money buying a bottle of liquid that is, on reflection, of quite inferior quality and complexity to a similarly priced whisky, rum, brandy, Tequila or gin. Or a similarly priced flat wine for that matter. But the truth is, in my opinion at least, Champagne is not worthy of either the reverence or the price tag that it receives.

With that little rant behind us, you might now be wondering what to do with that no-longer-so-appealing 'save it for a celebration' bottle of fizz that's been lurking in the kitchen for months now. The simple solution is to make a French 75. Or make a few. There are only a handful of decent sparkling wine-based cocktails known to mankind, and while I'd be happy to concede that the Bellini and Kir Royale are also both good drinks, the simplicity of their construction makes for a less than credible claim of cocktail-hood. The French 75 on the other hand is without doubt a cocktail, and perhaps the only cocktail containing sparkling wine that can truly be deemed delicious. Indeed, the ingredients in this drink don't just pair nicely with one another, they actually taste better than the sum of their parts. Gin, lemon and sugar syrup transform sparkling wine into the liquid that you'll end up wishing was in the bottle in the first place.

There's no genius behind this marriage of flavours – the drink is the forehead-slappingly obvious evolution of the Fizz and Sour. Here though, the wine takes the place of the soda. Sounds innocent enough, but when you consider a world where soda has an alcohol content in excess of 16%, you don't need to be a mathematician to realise that a French 75 packs a bit of a punch. Putting the theory to the test, after your third French 75 it becomes worryingly evident why the drink was named after a field gun. Used to great effect by the French during World War I, and more of a canon than a gun, 'Soixante-Quinze' fired noxious gas canisters the size of your forearm into enemy trenches. Perhaps it was the explosive and intoxicating effects of fizz and gin that caused Harry MacElhone, the bartender generally credited with the drink's invention, to name his cocktail after the most deadly weapon of the era.

TOM COLLINS

50 ML/1⅔ FL. OZ. OLD TOM GIN
25 ML/¾ FL. OZ. STRAINED FRESH LEMON JUICE
10 ML/⅓ FL. OZ. SUGAR SYRUP (SEE PAGE 17)
CHILLED SODA WATER, TO TOP UP
AN ORANGE SLICE, TO GARNISH

Add the gin, lemon juice and sugar syrup to a highball glass filled with plenty of cubed ice.
Gently stir with a barspoon while slowly topping up with soda.
Add more ice as required. Garnish with a slice of orange.

It's no secret that many of the best-known drinks out there have their origins in punches. The term 'punch' comes from the Hindi word for five (*panch*) and is thought to represent the five styles of ingredient that are essential to all punches: strong, long, sour, sweet and spice. It's a formula that is applicable to so many mixed drinks that it's a wonder punches aren't better recognised for what they are: cocktails in the embryonic stage of evolution.

Take the Tom Collins, for example. It's a drink that became very popular in late-19th century America, but it's actually based on an old English punch recipe. The history of the Tom Collins takes us back to some of the earliest gin punches, which featured on menus in some of Mayfair's legendary gentlemen's clubs, like Limmer's Hotel and the Garrick Club. In 1830, the bar manager of the Garrick Club was an American man called Stephen Price. He was an early advocate of iced soda water, which, when paired with gin, would have then seemed a strange combination. As David Wondrich notes in *Punch* (2011), 'soda water [was] a popular hangover cure… seen as an antidote to punch, not an accomplice'. The Garrick Club Punch recipe was published in The London Quarterly in 1835 and included 'half a pint of gin, lemon peel, lemon juice, sugar, maraschino, a pint and a quarter of water, and two bottles of iced soda water'. It became an international sensation.

Meanwhile, the bar at Limmer's Hotel on Conduit Street was being managed by a plump yet dignified head waiter by the name of John Collins. Collins had a handful of punch recipes up his tailored sleeves, but the most enduring of these – and the one that would later carry his name through every cocktail bar on the planet – was known simply as Limmer's Punch. The recipe was much the same as the Garrick Club drink, but instead of maraschino it used capillaire, a kind of sugar syrup that is aromatised with orange flower water.

Collins' drink also became recognised for its fizz, as well as its near-perfect balance of sweet, sour and aromatic elements. It was, and remains today, one of the best mixed drinks on the planet. As American cocktail culture took off through the mid-1800s, it was the reliable large-format serves, like Limmer's Punch, that got the single-serve treatment. And what better name for this sweet and sour fizzy delight than the name of its creator: John Collins. A John Collins called for the most popular gin in the US at the time, Holland's Gin (aka genever), but when the new, lighter style of London gin called Old Tom found its way to American shores (and genever fell out of fashion), John became Tom and the classic was born.

Unlike a Gin Fizz, which shares the same ingredients, a Tom Collins is built straight into a glass and simply stirred before serving. It's served with plenty of cubed ice, whereas a proper Gin Fizz should be served straight up. The absence of ice in the Gin Fizz means there's nothing to get in the way of wolfing the whole thing back in one satisfying gulp. A Collins however demands you take a bit more time.

GIMLET

60 ML/2 FL. OZ. PLYMOUTH NAVY-STRENGTH GIN
20 ML/⅔ FL. OZ. ROSE'S LIME CORDIAL OR FRESH LIME JUICE
A LIME WEDGE, TO GARNISH (OPTIONAL)

Shake all of the ingredients in a cocktail shaker with cubed ice and strain into a freezing cold martini glass then devour like you've just been diagnosed with scurvy. You may choose to garnish it with a wedge of lime, but I find one an unnecessary distraction.

Back in 1740 a British Admiral by the name of Vernon took the unprecedented step of watering down his sailors' rum rations with citrus juice. While initially (and quite understandably) not a hit with the men, this simple act went on to save countless lives. Seven years later, in 1747, a Scottish surgeon named James Lind discovered that incorporating fruit juice into the sailors' diets dramatically reduced the chances of them contracting a potentially lethal bout of scurvy. It turned out that scurvy was a result of vitamin C deficiency, so all ships began carrying citrus juice. In 1867 it became mandatory for British ships to carry lime juice rations.

The problem was that the juice tended to go off after a week or two sitting in a barrel. Another enterprising Scotsman, Lauchlan Rose, developed and patented a new method of preserving lime juice by concentrating it. Crucially though, the medicinal properties of the juice were retained and the vitamin C remained intact. Rose's Lime Cordial was born – the world's first concentrated fruit juice.

Drinking lime cordial on its own is no fun at all, so a (very large) spoon-full of gin is necessary to help the medicine go down. The story goes that it was Sir Thomas Gimlette, a surgeon in the Royal Navy, who allegedly introduced this drink as a means of inducing his messmates to take lime juice as an anti-scurvy medication. There's very little in the way of evidence to actually back this story up, though, and it's more likely that the drink simply takes its name from the sharp handheld tool used for punching holes

in things – a description that is just as apt for the drink as it is for the tool.

There's an elephant in the room among bartenders when it comes to mixing gimlets, and that is whether to use fresh lime and sugar, or lime cordial?

As we have already learned, the original calls for Rose's lime cordial, but the nomination of cordial was driven more by circumstance than by the pursuit of deliciousness. I'd wager lime juice would have been preferable if it were as practical and readily available as it is today. So with that in mind it's fair to consider a lime juice an upgrade. But this is beginning to sound a lot like a 'Gin Daiquiri', and in the Gimlet we have a cocktail that deserves its own name and its own terms and conditions. For me this is one occasion where nostalgia wins the day, and I'm happy to sacrifice a little freshness in a Gimlet to know that I am drinking a simple union of ingredients that have remained relatively unchanged for over 250 years. A win for Lauchlan Rose!

Now that we have settled upon the ingredients, ratio remains the final point of contention. *The Savoy Cocktail Book* (1930) suggests 50/50 gin and lime cordial, backed up by the 1953 Raymond Chandler novel *The Long Goodbye*, which stated that 'a real gimlet is half gin and half Rose's lime juice and nothing else'. But I urge you to consider what your dentist might say, and lower the lime cordial a little. Three parts gin to one part cordial is a sweeter (or not) spot to aim for.

LAST WORD

25 ML/¾ FL. OZ. GREEN CHARTREUSE
25 ML/¾ FL. OZ. MARASCHINO LIQUEUR
25 ML/¾ FL. OZ. BEEFEATER GIN
25 ML/¾ FL. OZ. FRESH LIME JUICE
25 ML/¾ FL. OZ. WATER

Add all of the ingredients to a cocktail shaker filled with cubed ice. Shake for 10 seconds then double-strain into a chilled martini glass. No garnish necessary.

These days, terms like 'Prohibition-era cocktail' and 'forgotten classic' get thrown around a lot by bartenders. Both labels are ridiculous, since cocktails were prohibited during Prohibition and because a truly forgotten classic would, by definition, still be forgotten (not documented in detail in a cocktail book like this!). But if there were a drink that qualified for both titles, it would have to be the Last Word.

The Last Word was first documented in Ted Saucier's saucily titled *Bottoms Up*, published in 1951. In the book – which features around a dozen suggestive illustrations of ladies posing with drinks – Saucier attributes the cocktail to the Detroit Athletic Club, adding that '[the] cocktail was introduced around here about thirty years ago by Frank Fogarty'. This timeline places the drink's creation during the early years of Prohibition (1920–33), which is quite something, since this cocktail would have required not one, not two, but three quite specific bottles of booze during a time when even moonshine was difficult to come by.

It turns out that the cocktail was actually invented around five years before Prohibition started, as it appeared on the Athletic Club's 1916 menu, a year after the place opened. The cocktail was listed at 35¢, making it the most expensive drink on the menu, probably on account of the Chartreuse. Apparently it was a popular drink, which is surprising because it

reads like a drunken teenage punchbowl on paper: two powerfully flavoured liqueurs, plus gin and lime. But, amazingly, it works a treat. Naturally, it's the Green Chartreuse that plays the leading role, delivering herbal and floral qualities in waves. The maraschino provides an alternate form of sweetness, with a touch of fruit and a little spice, while the gin hops and squeaks away somewhere underneath all that liqueur. Then there's the lime. Never before has citrus been so essential in a drink. Here, the lime cuts through the significant sweetness of the liqueurs, softens the alcohol and provides brightness where none existed before.

As an equal-part combination of five unrelated liquids, Last Word is the work of genius. Assuming you like Chartreuse, that is (otherwise you have no hope of enjoying it). If anything, the Chartreuse is the one ingredient of this drink that could and probably should be dialled down a touch. Its dominance is almost absolute, sometimes making it difficult to detect the maraschino and the gin at all, plus its impressive ABV (55 per cent) moves the drink from the 'approach with caution' category of cocktail straight into 'WARNING!'.

Adding a splash of water to the shaker helps dilute some of the concentrated character of the drink, and I'd recommend it, since you're going to need all the water you can get after a few of these.

MARTINEZ

50 ML/1⅔ FL. OZ. TANQUERAY GIN
25 ML/¾ FL. OZ. MARTINI ROSSO VERMOUTH
5 ML/1 TSP MARASCHINO LIQUEUR
3 DASHES OF DR. ADAM ELMEGIRAB'S BOKER'S BITTERS
ORANGE ZEST TWIST OR A MARASCHINO COCKTAIL CHERRY, TO GARNISH

Add all the ingredients to a mixing beaker and add cubed ice. Stir with a barspoon for
75 seconds, then strain into a chilled coupe and garnish as preferred.

This is the grandaddy of gin cocktails and the missing link between the dark spirited cocktails of the 19th century and the gin boom of the early 20th. The Martinez is a combination of gin, vermouth and bitters, usually with a splash of maraschino liqueur or orange curaçao. Now if that sounds a bit vague, it's because this is a vague drink and the bare-bones information I've just given you is about all we are certain of! The truth is that Martinez recipes vary wildly over the years, but it's partly the elusive nature of the drink that makes it so attractive – every time I drink one I wonder if this is the Martinez, or simply another variation of the concept.

The first thing that we can be sure of is that the Martinez and Martini are lookalike siblings. Born a few years apart in the late 1800s, the first-known reference to a Dry Martini is strikingly similar to that of a Martinez. The first reference to a Martinez in a cocktail book comes from O. H. Bryon's *The Modern Bartenders' Guide* (1884). Byron rather vaguely describes a Martinez as: 'Same as a Manhattan, only you substitute gin for whisky'. This wouldn't be too much of a problem if Byron hadn't listed two different Manhattan recipes in the same book and failed to mention which to use as a reference point. Both Manhattans are the same except one uses sweet vermouth instead of dry vermouth, which leads us nicely on to the crux of the matter. Should a Martinez be made with sweet or dry vermouth? The two cocktails are very different: dry vermouth creates, well, quite a dry cocktail, whereas a sweet vermouth Martinez is far bolder as the whisky and wine do battle in the glass.

Moving on, Jerry Thomas's revised edition of *The Bon Vivant's Companion* was published in 1887 with the Martinez recipe below, which is also vague on the vermouth front but fortunately, we are aware that in late 19th-century America, Italian (sweet) vermouth was far more common than French (dry) style.

TAKE 1 DASH OF BOKER'S BITTERS
2 DASHES OF MARASCHINO
1 PONY OLD TOM GIN
1 WINE GLASS VERMOUTH
2 SMALL LUMPS OF ICE

Shake up thoroughly, and strain into a large cocktail glass.
Put a quarter of a slice of lemon in the glass, and serve.
If the guest prefers it very sweet, add 2 dashes of the
gum syrup.

So, after around a decade's gap in recipes for the Martinez, the cascade of Prohibition-era cocktail books begin listing the drink once again. But this time there is a strong shift towards dry vermouth and a ratio of ingredients in greater favour of the gin. All in all this seems to point towards a style of Martinez moving towards that of the Dry Martini. So there we have it, inconclusive evidence on what exactly a Martinez is. The recipe given here is my personal favourite, and it's based entirely on a sweet Manhattan. Feel free to play around with it, invert the gin and vermouth, try dry vermouth, change up the bitters or hell, stick an umbrella in it if you think it'll make it right for you!

NEGRONI

30 ML/1 FL. OZ. GIN (AVOID CITRUS-FORWARD GINS, THEY GET LOST)
30 ML/1 FL. OZ. CAMPARI
30 ML/1 FL. OZ. NARDINI ROSSO VERMOUTH
GRAPEFRUIT ZEST OR AN ORANGE SLICE, TO GARNISH

A good Negroni should be served over big chunks of freezer-temperature ice, and there's nothing wrong with building the whole thing in a rocks glass. Stir for 1 full minute, then garnish with a small strip of grapefruit zest or a slice of orange, as preferred.

•

For new initiates it's wise to start with Aperol instead of Campari – it's like Campari's better-natured, mawkish cousin. If the bitterness is still too much you can always drop the ratio slightly, or do what I do and just up the gin!

It's a fairly well-kept secret that bartenders don't usually drink cocktails when sat on the receiving end of the bar, preferring instead to swig a beer or down a shot. It's an act of martyrdom, graciously sparing their fellow bartender the ordeal of cocktail mixing and the indignity of being observed by a keeper of the craft. The Negroni is one acceptable deviation from this rule however. Uncomplicated, yet challenging; strong, yet quaffable, the Negroni is hallowed ground to the bartender – an impeccable decoction of spirit, wine and bitter; blood red and ice cool.

If the significance of the Negroni should ever come in to question, one need only observe the openness of bar room discussion about the drink. Everyone has an opinion on its components, method of mixing, garnish and ice. And even though the brazen character of the Negroni may divide opinion, it is a drink that all cocktail enthusiasts desperately want to appreciate to its full extent. Regardless of preference, there remains a right of passage, or entitlement when it comes to the Negroni. Like your first face-scrunching sip of wine or beer, the conspiracy that surrounds this drink demands that you try, try again until life become incomplete without it. Here, in the Negroni, is the drink that, beyond all others, has become the Ferrari-red pin-up of the craft cocktail movement.

My understanding of the origins of the Negroni comes from the book *Sulle Tracce del Conte* (*On the Trail of the Count*) (2002) by Luca Picchi. Backed up by considerable historical documentation, it intimates that the drink is named after *deep breath* Camillo Luigi Manfredo Maria Negroni, who originally asked Fosco Scarselli, bartender at Café Casoni, to fortify his Americano (a bitter Italian aperitivo mixed with sweet vermouth and a splash of soda) with gin. This happened at some time in 1919 or 1920. One of the ways in which the story is qualified is by a letter sent from Frances Harper of London to [the evidently unwell] Negroni on October 13th 1920:

'You say you can drink, smoke, and I am sure laugh, just as much as ever. I feel you are not much to be pitied! You must not take more than 20 Negronis in one day!'

Nobody can drink that many Negronis in a single day, so it's fair to assume that the early version of the drink was either quite small or contained proportionately less gin – or both. These days we default to a Negroni made with equal parts gin, bitter liqueur/amaro, and sweet vermouth. The exact ratio can be tweaked (I prefer it slightly in favour of the gin, but with plenty of dilution) along with the brand of gin, bitter and vermouth. It's the simplicity of the drink coupled with the potential for customization that makes it a prevailing classic.

RAMOS GIN FIZZ

50 ML/1⅔ FL. OZ. TANQUERAY GIN
25 ML/¾ FL. OZ. DOUBLE/HEAVY CREAM
½ EGG WHITE
15 ML/½ FL. OZ. FRESH LIME JUICE
10 ML/⅓ FL. OZ. FRESH LEMON JUICE
15 ML/½ FL. OZ. SUGAR SYRUP (SEE PAGE 17)
A DASH OF ORANGE FLOWER WATER
A LEMON SLICE, TO GARNISH

Shake all the ingredients in a cocktail shaker with cubed ice for no less than 12 minutes.
Strain into a chilled highball glass and garnish with a slice of lemon.

Here is a drink that breaks the first rule of mixology: keep it simple. The Ramos Gin Fizz combines a multitude of ingredients, including cream and lemon, and comes with instructions to shake for no less than 12 minutes. However, the result is a silky smooth pick-me-up that, when balanced correctly, rivals any drink for pure sipping pleasure.

The drink dates back to 1888 New Orleans and a gent named Henry Ramos. Due to the low cost of labour back then, Ramos would hire 'shaker boys' to pump out the cocktails, and they would stand in a line continuously shaking. All night.

Taking a look at the ingredients list, this drink strikes me as a classic case of trial and error prevailing. There are few, if any, other drinks that contain both lemon AND lime juice; who knows why, as they certainly both have a unique flavour. There are even fewer drinks that contain citrus and cream together – that combo is pretty much universally accepted as a 'do not go there' throughout the bartending world. And then there is the addition of orange flower water, a unique ingredient that rarely appears in other mixed drinks. So surely the recipe must have been happened upon by chance? But what a day that must have been, as the finished product is an incredible achievement.

Expect to receive balanced refreshment and an oily consistency that slides down the gullet rather too easily. Sugar balances the sour as in a regular fizz, and the orange flower water adds a fragrant aromatic to accompany the gin. The first time I tasted a Ramos Gin Fizz, it immediately reminded me of my mum's lime cheesecake.

The shaking does a few things here: firstly, it cools and dilutes the drink. But after around a minute, the liquid reaches a plateau of temperature and dilution. The drink chills to around -2°C/28°F (depending on the ice used) and so the ice ceases to melt any more, but the drink will still stay cold. Minutes go by and not much changes at all. The other thing going on here is, of course, the mixing and emulsifying of the cream and egg. The egg acts as a surfactant, nicely combining the fat of the cream with the other ingredients into a silky smooth emulsion. To do this, the drink must be well mixed so that it doesn't split, although 12 minutes is probably a bit of overkill. This could, of course, be done prior to shaking with a blender, whisk or an ultrasonic probe, but hey, I guess it was cheaper to employ a bartender to do it back in 1888.

SALTED LIME RICKEY

50 ML/1⅔ FL. OZ. PLYMOUTH GIN
15 ML/½ FL. OZ. FRESH LIME JUICE
A SMALL PINCH OF SALT
CHILLED SODA, TO TOP UP
A LIME WEDGE, TO GARNISH

This drink needs to be cold – like, really cold. If possible use glasses from the freezer and make sure that your ice is dry. Fill a highball glass with chunks of ice; add the gin, lime and salt, then give it a good stir with a barspoon. While still stirring, pour the soda water in, leaving a small space at the top. Add more cubed ice, stir some more, then finish with a wedge of lime.

On page 57 of *Daly's Bartender's Encyclopedia*, published in 1903, a passage reads: 'This drink was devised by the late Colonel Rickey, whose fame as a congenial friend and dispenser of hospitality, as well as a judge of appetizing edibles and liquid refreshments, is world-wide, and it is universally conceded that for a drink containing an alcoholic ingredient it is the most refreshing known.'

This was the first book to publish a recipe for a Gin Rickey but, as the author alludes to, it was already a very popular drink by then and quite possibly the most popular gin-based cocktail of the 1890s. Today however, the Rickey is not known by many and very rarely called for, at least in my experience. It has faded into obscurity, and I'll be the first to admit that for a great deal of my early bartending career, I spared very little thought for the Rickey. It's a Collins or a Fizz made with lime juice, I thought. That's not to say I didn't think it was tasty – gin, lime and soda is a union of ingredients that makes as much sense on paper as it does swishing down your throat – but the thought of drinking one didn't exactly fill me with excitement. My opinion changed during a trip to India in 2011.

The Rickey is one of the most popular cocktails in India which, given the country's past dealings with gin and the favourability of its climate to citrus fruit growers, should come as no great surprise. But Rickeys are not made in the Western manner out there, oh no.

In India, there's either little or no sugar in the recipe and salt is added instead. Salt has the effect of buffering the acidity of the lime juice (in the same way as sugar), but also exposing some minerality from the gin and lime oil. Removing the sugar also makes the drink less cloying. Putting flavour to one side, forgoing the sugar altogether is an attractive proposition for some, making the drink a friend of diabetics and those counting calories. Although your doctor may question the logic of replacing sugar with salt, Indians swear by the drink's hydrating power during hot summer days.

The Rickey was probably first made with Bourbon, which is a little odd since Bourbon and soda are not especially enthusiastic bedfellows and it'll need a lot more than a squeeze of lime to change that. Nonetheless, George A. Williamson of Shoomaker's bar in Washington thought the marriage a loving one, and at some time in the 1880s conceived the Rickey, naming it after the Democratic lobbyist, Joe Rickey, who may or may not have had some part to play in the drink's creation. One thing is for sure, though: Rickey was quite displeased at having loaned his name to a popular cocktail, once saying that 'I was Col. Rickey, of Missouri, the friend of senators, judges and statesmen and something of an authority on political matters... But am I ever spoken of for those reasons? I fear not. No, I am known to fame as the author of the "rickey," and I have to be satisfied with that.'

SINGAPORE SLING

35 ML/1¼ FL. OZ. TANQUERAY GIN
15 ML/½ FL. OZ. CHERRY HEERING LIQUEUR
5 ML/1 TSP BENEDICTINE D.O.M. LIQUEUR
15 ML/½ FL. OZ. FRESH LEMON JUICE
2 DASHES OF ANGOSTURA BITTERS
CHILLED SODA, TO TOP UP
A LEMON SLICE, TO GARNISH

Build the ingredients into a chilled highball or sling glass filled with cubed ice, then give
it a quick stir with a barspoon and top with a splash of soda. Garnish with a slice of lemon.

It's fair to say that many folks class the Singapore Sling as a total abomination of a cocktail – a slaughtering of gin by sweet liqueurs, pineapple juice and toxic red syrups. I personally believe the Singapore Sling to be, at its best, a well-balanced refreshing cocktail with sweetness to balance a drying medicinal backbone. The drink was supposedly invented in the Long Bar at Raffles Hotel at some time between 1900 and 1920 (broad, I know), by a Hainanese-Chinese bartender called Ngiam Tong Boon. Raffles still include the following line on their cocktail list in the Long Bar:

Originally, the Singapore Sling was meant as a woman's drink, hence the attractive pink colour. Today, it is very definitely a drink enjoyed by all, without which any visit to Raffles Hotel is incomplete.

The term 'sling' had been applied to a mixed drink at least 100 years before that, but one of the earliest references to 'slings' in Singapore appeared in the Singapore newspaper *The Straits Times* on 2nd October 1903, in reference to drinks served at a morning send off for celebrity horse trainer, 'Daddy Abrams' on his voyage to Australia, where included on the menu was 'fizzy wine [and] pink slings for pale people'. Now, despite knowing that the early Singapore Sling was pink, a definitive Singapore Sling recipe from that time is not easy to come by. What we

know for sure is that it contained gin, lemon, soda and ice. It probably contained bitters. It likely had cherry brandy in it. It possibly had a touch of Bénédictine DOM liqueur in it, too. The main reason we believe all this stuff is down to a Straits Sling recipe in Robert Vermeire's 1922 book *Cocktails and How to Mix Them*:

This well-known Singapore drink, thoroughly iced and shaken, contains:

2 DASHES OF ORANGE BITTERS,
2 DASHES OF ANGOSTURA BITTERS,
THE JUICE OF HALF A LEMON
⅙ GILL OF BENEDICTINE
⅙ GILL OF DRY CHERRY BRANDY/½ GILL OF GIN

Pour into a tumbler and fill up with cold soda water.

Is it likely then that the Singapore Sling was originally called a Straits Sling and the name was later altered as a result of the drink's popularity in Singapore? Who knows? Raffles Hotel lost their original recipe at some time during the 1950s so now serve a drink developed by none other than the nephew of Ngiam Tong Boon. Given the similarities between the now commonly accepted Singapore Sling formula and Vermeire's 1922 one, it's possible that Boon's nephew simply took the earliest sling recipe he could find...

WHITE LADY

50 ML/1⅔ FL. OZ. GIN
15 ML/½ FL. OZ. COINTREAU
10 ML/⅓ FL. OZ. FRESH LEMON JUICE
10 G/⅓ OZ. EGG WHITE

Shake all of the ingredients in a cocktail shaker with cubed ice and double-strain into
a chilled coupe. No garnish necessary.

The White Lady belongs to that same family of cocktails as the Margarita, Sidecar and Cosmopolitan in that it's a modified sour, or as is the case, sweetened, by the inclusion of either triple sec or orange Curaçao (more on this shortly). This tradition of liqueur-ising classic sours dates back as far as the Brandy Crusta (see page 180), a drink invented in New Orleans in the 1840s and, in my opinion, the Ford Model T of cocktails.

There's just one slight problem with the New Orleans sour family of drinks, and that is they usually don't taste very good. Most often this is a fault of the bartender, who tends to refer to early-20th-century specifications of these drinks that call for too much citrus and too much liqueur modifier. The effect is something saccharine, flabby and altogether disagreeable, to the point where you find yourself taking great gulps of the cocktail so that the whole sorry business may be put to bed as quickly as possible. On the other hand, if you dial back the modifying ingredients slightly and allow the base spirit to shine, you can end up with a tasty, refreshing drink that's perfect as a pre-dinner sharpener.

The first documented recipe for the White Lady was published in Harry Craddock's *The Savoy Cocktail Book* (1930), and it's for that reason that the drink has an enduring association with the American Bar at the Savoy. But the American Bar is the most famous bar in cocktail history that didn't actually invent many classic cocktails (the trail runs dry after Hanky-Panky [see page 51] and Corpse Reviver No. 2 [see page 39], and the White Lady was not born there either. It was instead invented by one other famous Harry of the mixologists' stable – Harry MacElhone.

The son of a jute-mill owner from Dundee, Scotland, MacElhone began bartending at the age of 21, in 1911, at No. 5 Rue Daunou in Paris. Twelve years later, having worked through bars in New York and London, he would buy that bar and rename it Harry's New York Bar, which is today better known as simply Harry's Bar. It was while working at Ciro's Club in London that Harry first created a drink called White Lady.

Originally comprising two parts Cointreau to one part crème de menthe and one part lemon juice, the drink tasted like a bad throat lozenge and looked like that suspicious kind of swimming-pool water. It's a wonder he didn't lose his job. By the time he opened Harry's Bar in Paris, he had seen sense, removing the crème de menthe, knocking back the Cointreau and adding a healthy slug of gin. He also added some egg white, which besides giving the drink a foamy head, also produced a cool, white opacity that was like the visual equivalent of a snowball hitting you in the teeth.

This newly formulated White Lady, as with the White Lady recipe printed in *The Savoy Cocktail Book*, called for two parts gin to one part each of Cointreau and lemon juice. Craddock's recipe omitted the egg white. If you try a White Lady like this, you might find it's prone to all that flabby, saccharine regret – there's a whole shot of Cointreau in there, for goodness' sake! I suggest dialling them down a little and allowing the gin to do its thing. When you get it right, this is a wonderful drink, and the undisputed queen of the New Orleans sour family (for what it is).

HOLLAND HOUSE

50 ML/1⅔ FL. OZ. BOLS GENEVER
20 ML/⅔ FL. OZ. DRY VERMOUTH
10 ML/⅓ FL. OZ. FRESH LEMON JUICE
5 ML/1 TSP MARASCHINO LIQUEUR
LEMON ZEST, TO GARNISH

Shake all the ingredients with cubed ice and strain into a punch glass. Add an ice cube
from the shaker, or use a chunk of clear ice. Garnish with a twist of lemon zest.

Those readers old enough to remember the manned Moon landings might recall the Holland House brand of cocktail mixer. These popular bottles of 'Whiskey Sour' and 'Daiquiri' mix sought to simplify cocktail mixing at home by giving you all the ingredients you needed (except the alcohol) in one bottle. They saw quite a bit of success in the 1950s and 1960s until people realised that they tasted dreadful. And so began two decades of Dark Ages for the cocktail.

The Holland House serves as a handy mashup of at least four other classic gin cocktails I've included in this book. The first of those is the Martinez (see page 60) where the Holland House borrows vermouth and maraschino liqueur. The second is The Aviation, which sees gin combined with lemon juice and maraschino or violet liqueur (see page 36). The third is the Corpse Reviver No. 2 (favoured child of the Corpse Reviver family, see page 39), where we find gin, lemon, orange liqueur and dry vermouth in concert with one another. The fourth – if I may – is the Clover Club and you can turn to page 48 to discover the similarities for yourself.

All of the aforementioned drinks are, in isolation, quite different beasts, despite having a few similar ingredients. The Holland House is like a missing link between them all, probably pre-dating all but the Martinez. In fact, some cocktail buffs argue that the Holland House *is* a Martinez, given the similarities between the widely accepted modern recipe and Jerry Thomas' original Martinez recipe from 1862, which called for: maraschino, Old Tom gin, vermouth, bitters and a slice of lemon – forgo the bitters and up the lemon and you have yourself a Holland House right there. However a more likely explanation for the similarities between the two drinks is that most mundane of rationales: coincidence.

For the Holland House Cocktail (if you hadn't guessed already) it's the use of genever in place of gin that makes all the difference. The boldness of a nice oude genever or corenwijn, really stands up to the lemon and liqueur, while the vermouth offers some welcome dilution and finesse to the ensemble. I've heard the Holland House described as a 'malty Aviation' in the past, which is a fair description but also an injustice to a cocktail that deserves fair recognition in its own right, rather than loose comparisons to better known, classic cocktails (as I have just done).

PURL

1 LITRE/1 QUART BITTER (BRITISH ALE)
200 ML/6¾ FL. OZ. HENDRICK'S GIN
150 G/¾ CUP CASTER/SUPERFINE SUGAR
3 TSBP HONEY
1 TSP AMARILLLO HOPS (PREFERABLY, OR OTHER)
½ TSP DRIED WORMWOOD LEAVES
3 CLOVES
A 15-CM/6-IN. PIECE OF CINNAMON STICK
A LARGE PIECE OF GRAPEFRUIT ZEST

This recipe will give you 6 servings. Combine all the ingredients in a saucepan and heat gently to around 70°C/158°F, but do not boil. Keep the pan covered and ladle into mugs, cups or heat-resistant glasses for each guest.

It should come as no surprise that the Purl is a drink very close to my heart. After all, it's the name of the first cocktail bar that I opened!

It was my colleague Thomas Aske that came up with the name Purl for our bar – at the time, I had no idea what it was. Thomas had been reading Charles Dickens' *Sketches by Boz*, a collection of short stories depicting life in Victorian London. One section describes the actions of Londoners leaving the threatre:

One o'clock! Parties returning from the different theatres foot it through the muddy streets (...)retire to their watering houses, to solace themselves with the creature comforts of pipes and purl.

Further research dug up a reference to Purl in Dickens' *The Old Curiosity Shop*:

Presently, he returned, followed by the boy from the public house, who bore in one hand a plate of bread and beef, and in the other a great pot, filled with some very fragrant compound, which sent forth a grateful steam, and was indeed choice purl, made after a particular recipe.

Little did we know, however, that Purl had been around long before Dickens' time. Even as far back as the 17th century, in fact, when Samuel Pepys mentions Purl in one of his famous diary entries; he writes, 'Thence forth to Mr. Harper's to drink a draft of purle, whither by appointment Monsieur L'Impertinent...'

So what exactly is Purl? Well, it happens to be, in my eyes at least, one of the greatest warm winter pick-me-ups ever to grace a bar top. Choice spices and herbs combine with malty beer, bitter wormword and the botanical aromatics of gin to form a delicious concoction similar to mulled wine.

To create our bar's namesake, we set about trying various recipes, based on references in fictional works and other texts. However, I should say that not once, despite days of research, did I manage to find an actual recipe for Purl. Still hunting! So the recipe above is based on my own findings of how the ingredients combine and what spices best complement the beer and gin. The only certain rule that I could determine was that it had to contain beer, gin and wormwood – which, if you think about it, tenuously places the drink within the Martini family of cocktails.

VODKA

PERHAPS THE MOST VERSATILE OF SPIRITS
FOR MIXING, VODKA'S CLEAN TASTE MEANS
IT CAN ADAPT TO ITS SURROUNDING WITH
RELATIVE EASE, WHETHER IT'S IN A
RESTORATIVE MORNING-AFTER BLOODY
MARY OR THE 80S COCKTAIL REVIVAL'S
POSTER BOY, THE COSMOPOLITAN.

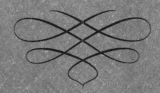

BLOODY MARY

50 ML/1⅔ FL. OZ. BELVEDERE VODKA
150 ML/5 FL. OZ. TOMATO JUICE (OF THE BEST-QUALITY YOU CAN LAY YOUR HANDS ON)
10 ML/⅓ FL. OZ. FRESH LEMON JUICE
ABOUT 3 DASHES OF WORCESTERSHIRE SAUCE
ABOUT 3 DASHES OF TABASCO
A LARGE PINCH OF SALT
A LARGE PINCH OF GROUND BLACK PEPPER
A CELERY STICK AND A LEMON SLICE, TO GARNISH

Shake (I like it that way) all the ingredients together in a cocktail shaker with cubed ice, then strain into a chilled highball glass. Garnish with celery and a slice of lemon.

The exact origins of the Bloody Mary are cause for much dispute. It's generally accepted that Fernand Petiot created the drink back in the 1920s while working at Harry's Bar in Paris. But it seems highly unlikely that the drink would have contained vodka, and probably would have been made with gin instead.

Which takes us to 1940s New York, where Petiot was working at the St. Regis Hotel. Allegedly, the manager of the hotel, Serge Obolensky, asked Petiot to spice up a vodka and tomato juice (comedian George Jessel popularized the unspiced version during the 1940s). Petiot added Worcestershire sauce, salt and pepper and a twist of lemon.

Of course, there's a solid argument in the fact that a Bloody Mary is simply spiced tomato soup sold cold and with vodka. The practice of vodka accompanying or featuring in savoury food is not a new one after all, with the most obvious being Russian borscht soup, made from seasoned beetroot/beets and sour cream. Pepper, spice and fresh acidity somehow greatly complement the neutral grainy backbone of vodka.

It's in the realm of the hangover cure that the Bloody Mary has made it's home – hey, it all but rules the realm! Taking a look at the key components, it's easy to see why it's such an obvious go-to. Vitamin C, salt, capsaicin and palate-coating viscosity. The greenery was, allegedly, a later addition to the concoction, when

at the Ambassador Hotel in Chicago a bartender spied a patron stirring her Bloody Mary with a stick of celery. Visually, it gives the drink a natural – it grew out of the ground like that – look about it, and sometimes that's all you need to make you feel human again...

One final note on making the drink. There is some debate around whether the mixture should be shaken, stirred, thrown or rolled. At some point in time a bright spark (second only to the person who said a similar thing about shaken gin Martinis) came up with the idea that commercially available tomato juice might in some way be 'bruised' by the action of shaking. Clearly they chose to ignore the fact that the tomato had already been picked, squashed, blended, filtered, heat concentrated, then rehydrated. And they must have concluded that tomatoes are the only fruit that can be bruised, since it's still ok to shake berries, citrus and pretty much anything else that grows on a tree or bush. Needless to say, tomato juice cannot be bruised, but the method of preparation CAN make a difference to the temperature, dilution and final viscosity of the drink, which are all important elements.

The ingredient that is all to often omitted from the melange is the lemon juice, yet it plays a crucial role in freshening up often bland cartoned tomato juice. You can press your own tomato juice, but it's a bit of a hassle, and actually produces a very different drink.

COSMOPOLITAN

40 ML/1⅓ FL. OZ. BELVEDERE CITRUS VODKA
20 ML/⅔ FL. OZ. COINTREAU
15 ML/½ FL. OZ. FRESH LIME JUICE
15 ML/½ FL. OZ. CRANBERRY JUICE
A FLAMED ORANGE ZEST, TO GARNISH (OPTIONAL)

Shake all the ingredients together in a cocktail shaker with cubed ice until ice cold,
then double strain into a chilled martini glass.

The Cosmopolitan really was the poster boy of the cocktail revival during the 1980s and 90s. It's iconic pale pink hue presented in a long-stemmed martini glass defines an entire era of cocktail culture and enjoyment of mixed drinks.

How has this drink remained on the tip of everyone's tongue for so long? Well, this might come as a shock, so brace yourselves – it's really very tasty. That is, when it's made correctly. The genius of a Cosmopolitan is that it combines all three of the major citrus fruits into one balanced drink. This fact is often overlooked, mainly due to the colour of the resulting liquid, which would have you believe that it's raspberry, strawberry or cranberry flavoured.

'But it is cranberry flavoured!' I hear you cry. No. It's cranberry coloured, that's all. A properly mixed Cosmo should contain only a small splash of cranberry, for a little colour and dilution. It's the other ingredients that are doing the heavy lifting here – citrus vodka, orange curaçao, lime juice.

Of course, the balanced flavour is not the draw for everyone, but it may well be the reason for repeat ordering. The fact that it shares its name with a popular fashion mag has done it no harm over the years. Neither has its seductive, oh-so-pink colour (ranging from salmon through to neon).

Back in the 80s, guests would order a Martini, just so they could hold a drink in a martini glass. Cheryl Cook, a bartender from Florida, recognised this in 1986, so created an approachable drink loosely based on a Cape Codder (vodka and cranberry), but with the addition of Rose's Lime Cordial and a splash of triple sec. Crucially, it was served in a martini glass. The drink was a big hit, but when Toby Cecchini, a New York-based bartender, got a hold of it, he tweaked it into the drink we recognise today. Lime cordial was removed and replaced with lime juice, the triple sec was upped and the cranberry reduced until the drink was a soft pale pink.

But the story doesn't end there. Toby Cecchini chose to garnish his Cosmo with a twist of lemon. These days we usually garnish with a flamed orange zest (see image on facing page) and it's another US bartender Dale DeGroff 'The King of Cocktails' who we have to thank for that. Dale has never revealed exactly where the idea came to him from, but the act of igniting oils from the surface of the orange skin and firing them on to the top of the cocktail turned the Cosmo into more than just a cocktail – now it was theatre.

The original cocktail was made with the then newly released Absolut Citron, but I much prefer the naturally macerated flavour of Belvedere Citrus.

BULLSHOT

400-G/14-OZ. CAN OF CAMPBELL'S BEEF BROTH (BOUILLON)
150 ML/5 FL. OZ. BELVEDERE UNFILTERED VODKA
150 ML/5 FL. OZ. WATER
30 ML/1 FL. OZ. FRESH LEMON JUICE
TABASCO, TO TASTE

This recipe will serve 4. Mix everything together in a pitcher and pour over cubed ice in a rocks glass. Give it a brief stir. If you wish, you can also experiment with other ingredients familiar to Bloody Mary: Worcestershire sauce, pepper, sherry etc.

If you're a fan of the Bloody Mary (see page 78) but always found it a touch too… *vegetarian* for your tastes, the Bullshot might be the meaty upgrade you've been searching for. As the name suggests, the Bullshot contains beef, or more specifically, beef broth. When does a cocktail cease being a cocktail and become simply beef stock with a splash of vodka in it? Well, right about now if you ask me, but given the bizarre level of popularity that the Bullshot enjoyed in the middle of the 20th century, it's difficult to argue against its status as a paid-up, card-carrying cocktail.

And how is such a drink conceived in the first place, you may ask? Not through the actions of a veterinary surgeon, I hasten to add, but through the ingenuity of a certain restaurant operator from Detroit. The year was 1952 and Lester Gruber's London Chop House (LCH) was not only one of the most popular restaurants in Motor City, but ranked as one of the best restaurants in North America. Frequented by celebrities like Aretha Franklin and barons from Detroit's booming motor industry, including Henry Ford II, LCH was *the place* to be seen eating and drinking. Drinks were not only of the carnivorous kind, mind you. The legendary LCH Pick-Up Drinks menu ran 9–11 every morning and included Old Pepper (rye whiskey, bourbon, hot sauces) and Kilroy's Bracer (Cognac, egg, anise) among its stimulants.

By the early 1950s, the place was so busy that Gruber opened a spillover bar across the road, called Caucus Club. And it was in this bar that Gruber became acquainted with John Hurley, a PR exec who was, at that time, fretting over a million cans of Campbell's Beef Broth that weren't flying off the shelves. At this time vodka was rapidly becoming the most popular drink in America, and Americans never grew tired of marvelling at how it could turn literally any liquid into an alcoholic one without altering the flavour of the original liquid. Beef broth was no exception.

The drink – served on the rocks with a twist of lemon – was known under various headings before Bullshot was settled on. Soup on the Rocks was one such moniker that was even marketed by Campbell's itself, albeit without the vodka (Campbell's was something of a family-friendly company). Other rejected titles included Ox on the Rocks and Matador. I would have gone for The Bovine Comedy.

In 1957, the Heublein Corporation, then owners of Smirnoff Vodka, got a hold of the drink and were running adverts in *Esquire* magazine for The Vodka Drink with Beef In It. By the early 60s the Bullshot had shot to international fame. The drink caught on in part because it was so left-field – enjoyed by those so cool that they could afford to be a little odd. Beef broth was also deemed to be something of a superfood back then. One *New York Post* journalist remarked that the drink was 'full of vitamins'. It took a few decades before people realised that salty broth was not going to grant everlasting youth and that no amount of vodka was likely to change that. By then, however, the Bullshot had already 'steak'd' its place in the history books.

BLUE LAGOON

30 ML/1 FL. OZ. BELVEDERE VODKA
20 ML/⅔ FL. OZ. BOLS BLUE CURACAO
15 ML/½ FL. OZ. FRESH LIME JUICE
CHILLED SAN PELLEGRINO LIMONATA (LEMONADE), TO TOP UP
AN ORANGE SLICE, TO GARNISH

Add the first three ingredients to a highball glass filled with cubed ice and stir for
30 seconds. Top up with more ice, then stir through the lemonade to fill the glass.
Garnish with a slice of orange.

Blue cocktails should really only be consumed in horizontal positions. They're kitsch, ridiculous and tend to be a lot of fun – ironically, not at all 'blue'. Blue drinks also have the potential to be quite delicious. Some people are surprised at this, and that's because they don't know what to make of blue as a flavour (see more on this on page 22). So, let's take a closer look at perhaps the bluest drink of them all – the Blue Lagoon.

The secret to this drink's colour is of course the blue Curaçao. Curaçao is an island in the Caribbean, off the coast of Venezuela. The island's name comes from the Portuguese word for 'healing', which came about after sailors who had contracted scurvy (vitamin C deficiency, see also the story behind the Gimlet on page 56) ate the fruit of the island and made miraculous recoveries. The Spanish introduced the Valencia orange to the island in the early 16th century, but it shrivelled, turned green and fell off the tree unripe in the dry Caribbean heat. This new orange (*Citrus aurantium currassuviencis*) became known locally as 'Laraha' and since it was too bitter to be eaten, it was instead used to make aromatic oils and liqueurs. Dutch colonists began to occupy Curaçao in the 1630s after the Dutch Republic declared independence from Spain. They brought the liqueur to Europe and called it Curaçao.

Nobody knows why blue Curaçao came into existence, but Bols Blue Curaçao had arrived in the US prior to Prohibition in the 1920s. There is evidence suggesting Bols sold various other colours of Curaçao at one time or another, indicating that blue was not the chosen colour, but just one colour among many. It happened to be the one that stuck, though.

By the 1950s, Bols had stepped up their sales strategy, expanding Blue Curaçao into the European market and selling it as a cocktail ingredient in the US. That's presumably what the Hawaii sales representative from Bols thought when he asked Harry Yee, the head bartender at the Hilton Hawaiian Village Waikiki, to design a blue cocktail in 1957. The subsequent Blue Hawaiian contained vodka, rum, blue Curaçao, pineapple juice, citrus and sugar. A more fitting name would have been Green Hawaiian, because mixing pineapple juice (which is yellow) with blue Curaçao (blue) gives you a green drink. Nice try, Mr Yee.

Around the same time, but on the other side of the Atlantic, Andy MacElhone (son of legendary bartender Harry MacElhone) thankfully developed a drink at Harry's New York Bar in Paris using the newly launched Blue Curaçao. MacElhone's drink was unmistakably blue, seeing as all the ingredients except the Curaçao were clear: gin, vodka, lemonade, lime juice and sugar. He called his drink the Blue Lagoon. Despite its gaudy appearance and daft name, the Blue Lagoon is in fact a perfectly tasty drink. The flavours here are all about citrus, with the holy trinity of orange, lemon and lime.

The Blue Lagoon is similar to the Cosmopolitan (see page 81) in this way, confusing you with a strange colour but in the simplest sense delivering a medley of citrus flavours. The recipe is adaptable, so feel free to adjust the balance of ingredients to suit your taste.

WHITE RUSSIAN

40 ML/1⅓ FL. OZ. BELVEDERE VODKA
20 ML/⅔ FL. OZ. COFFEE LIQUEUR (TRY CONKER)
20 ML/⅔ FL. OZ. DOUBLE/HEAVY CREAM

You can shake or stir this one, but I prefer to build it into the glass to avoid the foamy top.
Add all of the ingredients to a rocks glass and stir for 1 minute with plenty of cubed ice.

The White Russian is not a cocktail for everyone. It's a drink that underwent periods of huge popularity in the 1970s and again in the late 1990s, thanks largely to the The Dude in *The Big Lebowski*, who spends most of the movie mixing White Russians or drinking them (nine in total, though one of them ends up on the floor).

At the time of writing, however, the drink has fallen out of favour. Sickly coffee liqueur, anonymous vodka and gloopy cream are not appealing ingredients to a generation of drinkers that question provenance, sustainability and calorific content. Truth is, a White Russian is the drink uncool people order thinking that it makes them look cool. So like a shell suit or a lava lamp, perhaps it's time to unceremoniously load it into the back of a people carrier and send if off to the place where cocktails go to die.

But before we condemn the White Russian to the great plughole in the sky, it's worth highlighting two surprising things about this drink. The first is its history: there are 750 recipes in Harry Craddock's seminal 1930 work *The Savoy Cocktail Book*, but just four of them use vodka. Of those four recipes, two of them are drinks that contain crème de cacao. And of those two drinks one of them, called Barbara, contains vodka, crème de cacao and cream. Not quite a White Russian, of course – it's missing the all-important coffee liqueur – but not far off. Barbara was inspired by Alexander, which was originally a gin-based drink that first appeared in Hugo Ensslin's 1916 book *Recipes for Mixed Drinks*.

Coffee liqueur was first introduced to the commercial market in 1936, when Kahlúa was launched. It took some years for it to percolate its way into a cocktail

glass, the evidence of which appears in *The Stork Club Bar Book* of 1946, which lists another riff on the Barbara theme, named Alexander the Great. This drink combines crème de cacao, coffee liqueur, vodka and cream – a chocolate White Russian, if you will.

Logic would suggest that in the next part of the story somebody removed the crème de cacao and changed the name to White Russian? Well, not exactly. Remember there were two vodka drinks containing chocolate liqueur in *The Savoy Cocktail Book*? Well, the other one (not Barbara) was called the Russian Cocktail. This drink comprised equal parts vodka, gin and crème de cacao. It's a terrible drink, but it has a strong claim to being the precursor of the Black Russian (remove the gin and switch the crème de cacao for coffee liqueur), which was invented in 1949. The drink's inventor, Gustave Tops, who worked at the Hotel Metropole in Brussels, created this signature drink (comprising two parts vodka and one part Kahlúa) for Perle Mesta, the American ambassador to Luxembourg, who was hanging out in the bar.

As we move in to the 1960s, Alexander the Great and the Black Russian (this is beginning to sound like an epic saga) converged and the White Russian was born. The first mention of it can be found in California's *Oakland Tribune* on 21 November 1965. It featured in an advert for Southern Comfort's short-lived coffee liqueur, and the recipe called for '1 oz. each [of] Southern, vodka, cream.' With the history part out of the way, I guess you'll be wanting to know what the second interesting thing about a White Russian is? Well, here it is: it tastes great! Sweet coffee, unctuous cream and a nice boozy kick. What's not to like?!

LONG ISLAND ICED TEA

25 ML/¾ FL. OZ. BELVEDERE VODKA
25 ML/¾ FL. OZ. DON JULIO BLANCO TEQUILA
25 ML/¾ FL. OZ. BEEFEATER GIN
25 ML/¾ FL. OZ. APPLETON SIGNATURE RUM
25 ML/¾ FL. OZ. MERLET TRIPLE SEC
15 ML/½ FL. OZ. FRESH LEMON JUICE
CHILLED COCA-COLA, TO TOP UP
A LEMON SLICE, TO GARNISH

Add everything but the cola to a highball glass filled with cubed ice. Give a good stir,
mixing all of the ingredients thoroughly. Top up with more ice, then fill the glass with cola.
Garnish with a slice of lemon.

Here's a drink with no short measure of confusion surrounding it, which I guess is hardly surprising for a cocktail that contains five different base spirits. When I first cut my teeth as a bartender, I was told that the Long Island was a Prohibition-era drink. The inference being that it looked liked iced tea and was called iced tea, despite being most assuredly an alcoholic beverage that contained no tea at all. It was easy to imagine cops raiding a neighbourhood bar in New York's Long Island, and to their dismay discovering everyone sipping from tall glasses of what appeared to be iced tea.

This idea of an illicit, Prohibition-themed story behind the creation of the Long Island Iced Tea was later reaffirmed for me by the story of Old Man Bishop. This resident of Long Island, Tennessee, created a drink in the 1920s called – wait for it – Old Man Bishop that included rum, vodka, whiskey, gin, tequila and maple syrup. It seemed to me that the origin story was all tied up. But if you run a Google search asking 'Who invented the Long Island Iced Tea?', you're sure to encounter Robert 'Rosebud' Butt. This man claims to have come up with the cocktail in 1972 when working at the Oak Beach Inn on (of course) Long Island. He even has a website telling us so:

'I participated in a cocktail-creating contest. Triple Sec had to be included, and the bottles started flying.

My concoction was an immediate hit and quickly became the house drink at the Oak Beach Inn.'

Butt acknowledges that: 'Possibly similar concoctions were created elsewhere, at another time,' but what he doesn't acknowledge is *Betty Crocker's New Picture Cook Book*, published in 1961. This is where the first printed recipe for the Long Island Iced Tea can be found, and it was followed by appearances in the *American Home All-purpose Cookbook* of 1966 by Virginia T. Habeeb and in Punch in 1969. It seems Mr Butt might have been talking out of his… well, you get it.

As for the drink, it's coke and lemon juice, mixed with equal parts gin, rum, tequila, vodka and triple sec. Nearly everyone squirms at the thought of mashing these spirits together, which from a taste perspective I can certainly relate to. But if you are of the viewpoint that you are likely to become more drunk mixing these five base spirits than if you were to consume the equivalent volume of alcohol in a cocktail containing only one or two base spirits, I'm going to have to disappoint you. There's no proof that mixing drinks increases your level of drunkenness, or that it improves your chance of a hangover. What does cause drunkenness is drinking lots of alcohol in a short time, which is a practice that tends to go hand in hand with cross-discipline imbibing… and Long Island Iced Teas.

MOSCOW MULE

50 ML/1⅔ FL. OZ. SMIRNOFF BLACK VODKA
25 ML/¾ FL. OZ. FRESH LIME JUICE
10 ML/⅓ FL. OZ. GOMME OR SUGAR SYRUP (SEE PAGE 17)
100 ML/3⅓ FL. OZ. CHILLED GINGER BEER
A MINT SPRIG, TO GARNISH

Build the drink straight into a copper mug with cubed ice and garnish with a sprig of mint.

These days, it's 'the done thing' for a new brand of liquor to promote a selection of cocktails that best communicates the product's identity and flavour – a way of best utilizing the product, if you like. But it wasn't always that way. Go back 50 or so years and a new product would often find it very difficult to establish a foothold in a marketplace dominated by age-old, tried and tested brands. Launching a new spirit category was an even greater challenge, but that was what John G. Martin did with the Smirnoff vodka brand back in the 1940s.

Today it's hard to imagine a cocktail bar that doesn't stock vodka, but that's what it was like before the 1940s. *The Savoy Cocktail Book*, originally published in 1930, lists only two cocktails containing vodka out of around 800 drinks. Sure, people had heard of it, especially those seeking asylum from Russia after the revolution, but it was not a commonplace product (see Vodka Martini, page 93 for more background here). But by the 1980s, everyone was drinking vodka, and every cocktail bar was serving it – so what the hell happened? Rudolf Kunnett was a Russian-born businessman, living in Paris, who acquired a dying vodka brand from one Vladimir Smirnov. After failing to make a go of it, he sold the rights to John G. Martin of the Heublein spirits company in the US for $14,000. It was 1938. Heublein marketed the product as 'White Whiskey' – apparently after a mistake made when

corking the bottles – and the slogan 'It leaves you breathless' was born, cleverly promoting the clean flavour of the product along with reassurance that your spouse won't smell it on you after a daytime drinking session [ahem].

Sales weren't great to begin with, as apparently daytime drinkers hadn't taken to the product quite as planned. But in 1946, John Martin found himself in the Cock 'n' Bull pub on Sunset Boulevard, chatting to the proprietor who had made a similarly poor investment in ginger beer. John and Jack mixed the vodka with the ginger beer and capped it off with a squeeze of lime, then sourced copper mugs to serve it in (allegedly from another failed business-person), and the Moscow Mule was born.

Shortly after, the pair acquired one of the first-ever Polaroid cameras and then went from bar to bar photographing bartenders posing with bottles of Smirnoff vodka and copper mugs of Moscow Mule. They would show the Polaroid photographs to bar owners who didn't sell the product as a means of sealing the deal. Customers went nuts for the stuff and the vodka revolution had begun.

The drink was, for a very short time, called a Little Moscow, and the first 500 mugs were stamped as such. I own an original unopened bottle of Cock 'n' Bull ginger beer and dream of mixing it with a 1940s bottle of Smirnoff in an original copper mug. One day.

VODKA MARTINI

50 ML/1⅔ FL. OZ. BELVEDERE VODKA
10 ML/⅓ FL. OZ. DRY VERMOUTH
LEMON ZEST

Stir both ingredients over ice in a mixing beaker for at least 90 seconds. Strain into a frozen Martini glass. Twist a piece of lemon zest over the top to spritz the oils and discard the zest afterwards. I hate having lemon zest floating around in my Martini glass. It gets in the way and causes the second half of the drink to taste entirely of lemon. Don't do it!

At the turn of the 20th century, any American who had heard of vodka considered it a peasant's drink. *The Spatula*, a journal for pharmacists, wrote in 1905 '[that] the same kind of drink can be "enjoyed" by drinking the deadly spirits used in alcohol lamps'. It went on to conclude that '[vodka] may suit the Muscovite for the dead of winter, but in a climate like ours it could never become popular'. How wrong they were.

The first written reference to a vodka cocktail occurred in 1903, published in a New York-based Democratic periodical journal called *The Tammany Times*, where a fictional drunk Russian fisherman called Rumsouran Whisky engages with and destroys an imaginary Japanese fleet 'after soakin' in a couple train oil an' vodka cocktails to steady his nerve'. But since train oil (whale blubber) hardly counts as an ingredient, we'll revert to the first proper vodka cocktail, which made its entrance on the menu at the St Charles Hotel in New Orleans in 1911. Aptly named Russian Cocktail, this drink consisted of three parts vodka to two parts Russian cherry liqueur, and appeared in a little-known cocktail book called *Beverage Deluxe* in the same year.

Vodka maintained a vague yet fierce reputation up until the post-World War II period. Things would change quickly, though, as between 1950 and 1955 the quantity imported into the US increased from 50,000 cases to 5 million cases. Gin and whiskey were reliable spirits of an older generation, but easily substituted for this cool 'new' Cold War-era spirit. The Martini cocktail was near the front of the queue/line for this treatment.

The first reference to a Vodka Martini is in David A. Embury's *The Fine Art of Mixing Drinks* (1948) in which a recipe for a Vodka Medium Martini mixed with both French and Italian vermouth and apricot brandy is offered. He mentions that vodka can be substituted for gin in a classic Martini, at which point you have a Vodka Martini. In Ted Saucier's 1951 book *Bottoms Up*, the same drink goes under the guise of a Vodkatini and calls for '⅘ jigger Smirnoff vodka [and] ⅕ jigger dry vermouth', with a twist of lemon peel as a garnish. In later editions of Embury's book, the same Vodka Martini is referred to as a Kangaroo, though nobody has yet worked out where the link to the marsupial comes from... However, the 1950s literature that had a bigger influence over the Vodka Martini's rise to fame was found in the fiction section. James Bond is synonymous with the Vodka Martini, though the movie adaptations hugely overstate Bond's attachment to the drink. He was a heavy drinker, but his preference was more towards whisky and Champagne. That said, he drinks neat Wolfschmidt vodka with M in *Moonraker* (1955), where he drops black pepper into the glass, stating that, 'In Russia, where you get a lot of bathtub liquor, it's an understood thing to sprinkle a little pepper in your glass. It takes the fusel oil to the bottom.'

In the first Bond novel, *Casino Royale* (1953), Bond asks the bartender to mix a Vesper Martini (gin, vodka and Kina Lillet) but he drinks his first true Vodka Martini in the second novel *Live & Let Die* (1954), in which Fleming provides the recipe at the end of the book (six parts vodka to one part vermouth, shaken).

ESPRESSO MARTINI

50 ML/1⅔ FL. OZ. BELVEDERE VODKA
20 ML/⅔ FL. OZ. BREWED ESPRESSO COFFEE
10 ML/⅓ FL. OZ. SUGAR SYRUP (SEE PAGE 17)

Shake all the ingredients together in a cocktail shaker with cubed ice and strain into
a chilled martini glass. Resist the urge to garnish with coffee beans.

Back when I first cut my teeth as a cocktail bartender, when bigger cocktail lists were better and flaming an orange twist was regarded as innovative, the Espresso Martini was the height of cool. Caffeine, alcohol, sugar. Everything the body needs for a good night out, and all held together by our 1980s superhero, the martini glass.

The Espresso Martini is based on a drink created by the UK's crown prince of cocktails, Dick Bradsell while he was working at the Soho Brasserie. The story goes (and it does vary depending on who you ask) that an attractive female model approached the bar where Dick was working and asked him for a drink that would 'pick me up, then f**k me up' – if only all drink requests came with such exact requirements. Dick eyed the bar's shiny new espresso machine and promptly mixed vodka, espresso and sugar together, then served it in a martini glass. The Espresso Martini was born.

The growing popularity of espresso coffee in the 1980s and 90s made the Espresso Martini an inevitability. The espresso in the drink achieves three things at once: first, it masks the alcohol in the vodka; second, it gives a caffeine kick to the receiver; and third, it turns the drink a stunning opaque brown. Also, if you use a good-quality coffee and extract the espresso correctly, you'll be rewarded with a pale foamy head, produced by the CO_2 bubbles dissolved in brewed coffee. Serve an Espresso Martini in a half-pint glass and it really does look like a Guinness!

WHISKY/WHISKEY & BOURBON

ALTHOUGH TOP-SHELF BOTTLES LEND
THEMSELVES TO BEING SAVOURED STRAIGHT,
WHISKY/WHISKEY DRINKS ARE STAPLES
ON ALL COCKTAIL BAR MENUS AS THIS
AMBER SPIRIT PROVIDES THE BACKBONE TO
CLASSICS SUCH AS THE MANHATTAN AND
OLD FASHIONED AND BREATHES THE LIFE
INTO A REFRESHING MINT JULEP.

WHISKY SOUR

50 ML/1⅔ FL. OZ. SCOTCH WHISKY
25 ML/3/4 FL. OZ. FRESH LEMON JUICE
12.5 ML/SCANT 1 TBSP SUGAR SYRUP (SEE PAGE 17)
½ AN EGG WHITE (OPTIONAL)
A MARASCHINO COCKTAIL CHERRY AND A LEMON SLICE, TO GARNISH

Shake all the ingredients together in a cocktail shaker with cubed ice. Strain into a mixing beaker and blitz briefly with a stick blender or aerolatte. Pour into a rocks glass and garnish with a cocktail cherry and a slice of lemon.

Most recipes for a sour with whisky in them would include the letter 'e' in whisk(e)y, denoting the origin of the liquor to be American (bourbon and rye) or Irish. Scotch whisky is not the norm for a sour, but not wholly unheard of either. I've chosen to use Scotch here for one simple reason – it tastes really good. That's not to say that this drink doesn't work well with bourbon, rye, Irish, Indian, Welsh, English or Japanese whiskey, too – or in fact virtually any other spirit – but the Scotch whisky sour deserves a bit of recognition in my opinion.

The Sour is one of the staple cocktail families – not particularly exciting in itself, but an essential part of the cocktail demographic. Sours are the basis for other families of drink, such as Fizzes (a Sour shaken and topped with soda), Collins (a Sour stirred with soda), Rickeys (a lime Sour topped with soda) and the family that the Sidecar, Cosmopolitan and White Lady belong to. They are simple, dependable creatures that there is no shame enjoying from time to time.

Jerry Thomas's 1862 *How to Mix Drinks* or *The Bon Vivant's Companion* was the first cocktail book to publish a Sour recipe, five in fact, including the Whiskey Sour (with bourbon), Gin Sour, Brandy Sour, Egg Sour (with brandy and curaçao) and Santa Cruz Sour (with rum). The Whiskey Sour reads:

Take 1 large teaspoonful of powdered white sugar, dissolved in a little seltzer or Apollinaris water. The juice of half a small lemon. 1 wine glass of bourbon or rye whiskey. Fill the glass full of shaved ice, shake up and strain into a claret glass. Ornament with berries.

This formula has remained almost untouched over the last 150 years and there's a very good reason for that – it works. Thomas's recipe calls for the reader to mix a water/sugar solution on the fly, but these days we use sugar syrup or gomme. The combination of spirit, lemon juice and sugar syrup in a 4:2:1 ratio results in a balanced drink most of the time, every time.

Why Scotch? Well, Scotch and lemon juice have as strong an affinity as any two ingredients I can think of (see exhibit A – the Hot Toddy), there's something medicinal about the pairing. I also love the way the malt and peaty (if applicable) notes shine through, softened by the sweet and sour balance, but still more than apparent. In fact, I've found that a Whisky Sour is an excellent tool for initiating non-Scotch drinkers into the balmy folds of malt whisky appreciation.

BLUE BLAZER

120 ML/4 FL. OZ. DEWAR'S 12-YEAR-OLD BLENDED SCOTCH WHISKY
120 ML/4 FL. OZ. BOILING WATER
2 TSP SUGAR
LEMON ZEST, TO GARNISH

Although this drink can be made using steel pitchers (the kind that might be used for steaming milk in a café) you will find it easier and safer to use large tankards with nice, long handles. This recipe makes 2 servings.

•

Preheat both tankards with hot water, then put the whisky in one tankard and the boiling water and sugar in the other. Light the whisky (this may take a couple of attempts if the whisky is cold) and swirl it around in the tankard to encourage a good flame. Pour the burning whisky into the tankard with the water. Then pour back, repeating the process. As the liquids warm, the flames will become more ferocious. Practice will allow you to increase the distance between vessels when pouring, giving the effect of a long, blue-flamed waterfall. You can snuff out the flame at any time by covering the flaming vessel with the base of the other vessel. Pour into a handled glass and serve with a twist of lemon zest. Do this taking all the necessary safety precautions.

The 19th-century mixologist was considered a master of all things delicious and fancy. But 'fancy' in the 1800s didn't mean dry ice and strips of orange zest cut with pinking shears. The original mixologists had more theatrical tricks up their sleeves and it's in part thanks to these feats of alcohol entertainment that the art of bartending achieved celebrity status.

Jeremiah 'Jerry' P. Thomas is the undisputed father of American mixology. As a travelling bartender he worked across dozens of bars through the 1850s in St Louis, Chicago, Charleston, New Orleans and New York. His *Bar-Tender's Guide* (alternately titled *How to Mix Drinks* or *The Bon-Vivant's Companion*), published in 1862, was the first cocktail book written by a US author, and the first book to successfully categorise the vast array of mixed drinks that had been born out of the early 19th century. Most of Thomas's category systems are still in use today, and the creation of numerous classic cocktails are credited to him as well.

Perhaps his most famous creation is the Blue Blazer, which he developed while working at the El Dorado gambling saloon in San Francisco. Using a set of large, solid-silver mugs, Thomas would 'throw' flaming slugs of burning Scotch between the vessels to an audience of mesmerised patrons. In the *Bar-Tender's Guide*, he noted that any patrons witnessing the display, 'would naturally come to the conclusion that it was a nectar for Pluto [god of the underworld] rather than Bacchus'.

When I opened my first London bar in 2009 we put a Blue Blazer on the menu. Being a speakeasy kind of place, where bartenders wore bow ties and guests read menus by candlelight, it fitted in rather well. But the bar was a rabbit warren, meaning that only around 20 guests at any one time had a clear view of the drink's preparation. This was problematic in so far as the Blue Blazer was concerned, since much of the enjoyment of the drink is to be had admiring the knife-edge spectacle of its preparation. So we took to pouring Blazers at the table. The combination of danger and the promise of alcohol was enough to excite even the most sceptical, but for me it offered a taste of just how mind-blowing such a performance must have seemed 150 years ago.

BOULEVARDIER

40 ML/1⅓ FL. OZ. MAKER'S MARK BOURBON WHISKEY
20 ML/⅔ FL. OZ. CAMPARI
20 ML/⅔ FL. OZ. MARTINI ROSSO VERMOUTH
ORANGE ZEST, TO FINISH AND GARNISH

Add all of the ingredients to a mixing beaker and stir over cubed ice for at least 90 seconds.
Strain into a chilled coupe, spritz the oils from a small piece of orange zest
over the top and use it as a garnish.

If the recipe for this drink seems familiar, that's because it is. The Boulevardier is the American cousin of the Negroni, made from a base of American whiskey and named for an American… in France.

This drink, like many others, was created by Harry MacElhone of Harry's New York Bar in Paris. It is mentioned only briefly in his book *Barflies and Cocktails* (1927), not among the cocktail recipes, but rather in the epilogue that follows, which recounts the antics of his regular patrons: 'Now is the time for all good barflies to come to the aid of the party, since Erskine Gwynne crashed in with his Boulevardier Cocktail: ⅓ Campari, ⅓ Italian vermouth, ⅓ bourbon whisky.' Erskine Gwynne was a wealthy young journalist who came to Paris from New York, and in 1927 launched a literary magazine for posh men about town called – you guessed it – *The Boulevardier*. On appearances this seems like a straightforward origin story: a famous cocktail bartender with his own written account of the drink's creation and a catchy name attributed to a known journalist… but there are just a couple of outstanding matters.

The first question that needs addressing is how did Harry MacElhone come to have bourbon in his bar in 1927? Prohibition did not exist in France at that time, of course, but spirits production in the US had been on hold for nearly a decade, and the only whiskey produced there was for medical purposes. The only answer is that MacElhone had gathered quite a stock of the stuff prior to the 1920s and must have charged a high premium for drinks that contained it.

The second curiosity here is the drink itself. It shares more than a passing similarity to the Negroni, leading many drinks experts to conclude that it was based on the Negroni, which was invented in Florence sometime around 1919 or 1920. Harry MacElhone published an earlier book called *Harry's ABC of Mixing Cocktails* (1919), but as one might expect, there's no mention of the Boulevardier or the Negroni in there. There's also no mention of the Negroni in *Barflies and Cocktails* (1927), and indeed you have to wait until 1959 and *Wake Up In Europe: a Book of Travel for Australians & New Zealanders* by Colin Simpson before we see the first mention of the Negroni in print.

However, looking at the 1922 reprint of *Harry's ABC of Mixing Cocktails*, we do encounter a new cocktail that contains equal parts whiskey, Campari and vermouth. In this instance, the drink is made with Canadian whiskey and French vermouth. The name of the drink is Old Pal. Incredibly, Harry attributes the creation of Old Pal to another American journalist living in Paris, as we can see with the credit: 'Recipe by "Sparrow" Robertson, Sporting Editor of the *New York Herald*, Paris.'

In summary, the whole thing is a bit of a mess. But messes are not uncommon where the documentation of alcohol is concerned. It goes without saying that a lot of what gets written about drinks is done so while the author is under the influence – yours truly being no exception. But taking all that we know about Harry's meddling with Campari, vermouth and whiskey in the 1920s, I think it's fair to say that both the Old Pal and

the Boulevardier cocktails were created completely independently of the Negroni. That leaves one final (rather important) question: is the Boulevardier a good drink?

Well, the great thing about using bourbon in place of gin is that, unlike the delicate juniper characteristics of the latter, the aged spirit is actually discernible in the finished drink. I like a Negroni as much as the next bartender with a tattoo of a bitters bottle on their neck, but picking out the gin in an equal-parts Negroni is nigh on impossible. Not so with a Boulevardier. That said,

I still think it pragmatic to up the amount of bourbon a little to really let it shine. This shifts the cocktail further in the direction of a Manhattan. Indeed, if you were to draw a Venn diagram with circles that represented a Negroni and a Manhattan, the Boulevardier would sit in the intersection.

With that kind of pedigree behind it, it's quite puzzling that the Boulevardier hasn't progressed beyond the realms of the late-night, post-shift bartender-to-bartender order and into the domain of regular drinkers. Try it!

MANHATTAN

50 ML/1⅔ FL. OZ. WOODFORD RESERVE BOURBON WHISKEY
25 ML/¾ FL. OZ. MARTINI ROSSO VERMOUTH
2 DASHES OF BOB'S ABBOTTS BITTERS
A MARASCHINO COCKTAIL CHERRY OR ORANGE ZEST, TO GARNISH

Stir all the ingredients together in a mixing beaker with cubed ice for 1 minute, then strain into a chilled coupe. Garnish with a Maraschino cocktail cherry or a small twist of orange zest, as preferred.

There are a few reasons why the Manhattan can claim to be one of the most iconic cocktails in the world, the most obvious being that it is named after one of the world's most famous metropolitan islands. Another reason is that it has placed itself in the same social circle as the golden girl herself, the Martini. In fact, some might say the Manhattan is to Ken as the Martini is to Barbie. The final, and most important reason of all, is that it tastes absolutely fantastic! The Manhattan is my go-to drink, a get-out-of jail-free card when decision making seems too much like hard work and all I really want is something that is familiar and tasty – a comfort blanket of corn and wine, if you will.

There is a popular story associated with the creation of the Manhattan that is more than likely untrue. But the story is such a good one that I'll tell it anyway, since, and I think you'll agree, it really ought to be true! The story goes that one Dr. Ian Marshall invented the drink in 1874. Apparently, he was attending a banquet hosted by Jennie Jerome (aka Lady Randolph Churchill – Winston Churchill's mother) at the Manhattan Club in NYC. The banquet was being held to honour presidential candidate Samuel J. Tilden. Allegedly, the drink was a great success and as word spread guests in other bars began ordering the cocktail made famous at the Manhattan Club.

Sadly, there is a big problem with that story. On the date of the supposed banquet, Lady Randolph Churchill was actually in Blenheim, England, christening her newly born son, Winston – a factual inconvenience, since it would be fitting that such a great drinker was linked to such a great drink.

It is a strange thing that you can take virtually any spirit, mix two parts of it with one part sweet vermouth, add a dash of bitters and be confident in the knowledge that it'll probably taste pretty damn good. With Cognac it's called a Harvard (see page 187), with Gin it's a Martinez (see page 60), with Scotch it's a Rob Roy (see page 114) and so on. Perhaps none work so well as the Manhattan, though.

Some folks believe that a Manhattan should be made with rye in place of bourbon. I have listed the latter, since its more readily available, but, as with most cocktails, it really comes down to personal choice, with the rye being a little more spicy and perhaps a little more 'man-ly'.

MINT JULEP

50 ML/1⅔ FL. OZ. OLD SCOUT BOURBON WHISKEY
10 ML/⅓ FL. OZ. SUGAR SYRUP (SEE PAGE 17)
12 MINT LEAVES, PLUS SPRIGS TO GARNISH

Add all the ingredients to a julep tin or rocks glass and use a barspoon to churn well with crushed ice. Add more ice as necessary and garnish with a couple of sprigs of slapped mint (to release the aroma). Add straws if drinking from a rocks glass.

The word julep derives from the Persian word 'gulab', meaning rosewater. In the 18th century, juleps became a popular type of medicinal cordial, intended to treat stomach complaints. All types of herbs and spices were infused into them, along with sugar and sometimes alcohol. What differentiates a julep from other sorts of medicinal infusions is that all of the ingredients were soluble and the resulting liquid transparent. Through my research, I discovered a 1791 book, published in Edinburgh, Scotland, called *Domestic Medicine* that included a recipe for a 'Musk Julep' that called for spirit, musk, cinnamon and peppermint water. It was designed to get rid of hiccups.

Over in the US, however, juleps were beginning to find a fanbase as a morning pick-me-up. The mint julep was first referenced in print in 1803 by British traveler John Davis, who mentioned a beverage he drank at a Virginia plantation. Davis described the drink as 'a dram of spirituous liquor that has mint steeped in it, taken by Virginians of a morning'.

Julep is synonymous with the Kentucky Derby, the annual thoroughbred horse race held in Louisville, Kentucky. Over the course of the Kentucky Derby weekend, the Churchill Downs race track make an estimated 120,000 mint juleps for spectators. The Derby Museum reports that the mint julep became Churchill Downs' signature drink in 1938, the year they began serving it in souvenir glasses for 75 cents.

Like many of the most enduring drinks, the julep is a drink that requires patience and preparation. But in the picking of mint, preparing of the ice, and the slow stirring of bourbon we find a ritual that builds anticipation amongst the lucky recipient. A julep that's simply handed to you five seconds after placing the order will never taste as good as the one you had to wait for. Also, like nearly all of the best drinks, the julep is fiendishly simple: whiskey, mint, sugar, ice. That's it! And being so simple means it's wide open to customization too. Making crushed ice out of sweet tea is one of my favorite modifications of this cocktail.

A julep is traditionally served in a julep tin with a julep strainer placed on top. This drink pre-dates the modern use of straws in cocktails, and while the crushed ice holds the mint in place, you still need something to stop the crushed ice from falling all over your face.

RUSTY NAIL

40 ML/1⅓ FL. OZ DEWAR'S 12-YEAR-OLD SCOTCH WHISKY
20 ML/⅔ FL. OZ. DRAMBUIE

Take a big lump of ice, pop it in a rocks glass, then pour the whisky and Drambuie
over the top and stir well for a minute. That's it.

If you can't make a Rusty Nail taste good it's probably time to give up on this mixology thing. After all, a drink that comprises only two ingredients, where one of them is Scotch whisky and the other is Scotch whisky that's been sweetened and had herbal flavours added to it ought to be simple enough to balance to anyone's palate. Like it sweeter? Add more Drambuie. Like it dryer? Use less Drambuie. Only those people born with a complete inability to understand why they do or do not like a flavour or with an inability to change things appropriately will stand a chance at messing this one up.

So what is this Drambuie stuff? In the most basic sense it's a whisky liqueur, flavoured with heather honey, a bunch of other herbs and exotic spices. The name Drambuie is derived from Scots Gaelic *an dram buidheach* and means 'the drink that satisfies'. By the light of an open fire on a cold Scottish evening, it'll do just that.

The accepted history of this product is a tale of Scottish spirit seasoned liberally with various fantastical components. It begins with Bonnie Prince Charlie (Charles Edward Stuart) aka the Young Pretender, whose failed Jacobite uprising of 1745 left him in exile on the Isle of Skye rather than sitting on the thrones of England, Scotland, Ireland and France. With little left to occupy his time, Charlie became acquainted with the noble arts of wenching and drinking – French brandy being his preferred tipple. As was common amongst the nobility of that time, Bonnie Prince Charlie had his own recipe for a curative

liqueur, which would have been formulated for him by a personal physician or apothecary. The story goes that Charles shared the recipe for his tonic with his friend Captain John MacKinnon in 1746, though Drambuie's testimony on this matter has changed at least twice over the years. Early-19th-century advertising states it was 'a follower of Prince Charlie' that brought the spirit to Scotland, then later a 'gentleman of the bodyguard of Prince Charlie'.

The truth is that nobody really knows how John MacKinnon came to acquire the recipe, but most people agree that it was probably brandy-based in the first instance. The recipe remained a MacKinnon family secret for some 150 years, then was passed on to the Ross family who ran the Broadford Hotel on the Isle of Skye. The Rosses registered the trademark for Drambuie in 1893. Production later moved to Edinburgh and the company was bought by Malcolm MacKinnon (no relation to the other MacKinnons in this tale), in whose family it has remained ever since.

These days, Drambuie has a reputation for being a divisive liqueur. I have friends and colleagues who love it and others who hate it, but very few who sit on the fence. The general rule of thumb, so much as I can tell, is if you're not averse to very sweet things, you will get along with it just fine. This, then, is where the Rusty Nail comes into its own. A simple tweak of the ratios will get you where you want to be in terms of sweetness and herbal lift.

PICKLEBACK

50 ML/1⅔ FL. OZ. JAMESON IRISH WHISKEY
50 ML/1⅔ FL. OZ. DILL PICKLE JUICE

Pour the two liquids into separate shot glasses.
Shoot the whiskey, then the pickle juice. That's about it!

I was first introduced to the phenomenon of the Pickleback by James 'Jocky' Petrie of The Fat Duck restaurant. He was sitting at the bar in Purl (my first London bar) one evening and after a couple of drinks started raving about a mad drink that combined Irish whiskey and pickle brine. It sounding both disgusting and fascinating, so I immediately sent the barman back out to the shop to buy a jar of dill pickles. Jocky instructed us to pour Irish whiskey into one shot glass and the juice from the dill pickle jar into another. You shoot back the whiskey, then chase it with the sweet-and-sour pickle brine. It was amazing.

So how does it work? It would appear that the intense sweet, sour and saltiness of the pickle juice does a very good job of detracting from the alcohol burn of the whiskey. But not only that, it actually couples nicely with the liquor, leaving a kind of sweet, toffee-apple aftertaste that is far from unpleasant. The ritual is not dissimilar from that of the Tequila and Sangrita (see page 174), which achieve much the same thing, albeit with very different flavour combinations.

Now I must confess at this stage to being an Irish Pickleback advocate, which is not necessarily true to the historical roots of the drink. It was T. J. Lynch of NYC bar Breslin who, in 2009, made a Pickleback with Jameson whisky famous, but it would appear that the practice had been going on with bourbon for at least a year or two before that. According to New York bartender Toby Cecchini (famed for his part in the creation of the Cosmopolitan), the drink was first served to him in 2007 with Old Crow Bourbon at the Bushwick Country Club in the Williamsburg neighbourhood of Brooklyn. It seems that the ritual may have been inspired by a culture of chasing liquor with pickle juice adopted by Texan long-haul truck drivers. The salt supposedly helps keep you hydrated, thus preventing a morning-after trucker headache. Since Texas borders Mexico, it seems plausible that the idea originally came from the Sangrita.

Either way, the quality of the pickle juice is far more important than the quality of the whiskey, since the ritual is designed to clear the palate of low-grade liquor, so choose your pickles wisely!

WHISKEY HIGHBALL

40 ML/1⅓ FL. OZ. KOVAL FOUR-GRAIN WHISKEY
120 ML/4 FL. OZ. ICE-COLD SODA WATER
A LEMON SLICE, TO GARNISH

Add the whiskey to a chilled highball class filled with cubed ice and stir briefly. Top up with the soda and give it another, brief, gentle stir. Garnish with a slice of lemon.

I'm a big believer in highball drinks and consider them one of the best entry routes into whiskey appreciation. There aren't many things I like more than sipping on a nice rye or single malt and appreciating the distinctions of its crafting, but one of the things I do like just as much is enjoying an ice-cold, effervescent highball on a warm afternoon.

The origins of the drink are actually English. The original highballs were brandy-based drinks that became popular in Europe in the mid-19th century. Then, when Scotch whisky came into vogue, it supplanted brandy as the base spirit. New York barman Patrick Duffy claimed the highball was brought to the US in 1894 from England by actor E. J. Ratcliffe (1863–1948). Duffy wrote, in his 1934 *The Official Mixer's Manual*, that, 'it is one of my fondest hopes that the highball will again take its place as the leading American Drink'.

The drink achieved peak popularity in the mid-20th century, when it appeared regularly on British television and was consumed by everyone from Winston Churchill to James Bond (who in the Fleming novels drank more highballs than he did Martinis). It didn't ever regain the popularity in the US that Duffy hoped for, and until quite recently has fallen out of fashion in the UK, too.

That is set to change though. I believe that highballs are the next big thing in mixed drinks. Don't believe me? Well how about you make one and tell me how good you think it is…

ROB ROY

**50 ML/1⅔ FL. OZ. SCOTCH WHISKY
25 ML/¾ FL. OZ. MARTINI ROSSO VERMOUTH
2 DASHES OF ORANGE BITTERS
A DASH OF SUGAR SYRUP (SEE PAGE 17), OPTIONAL
ORANGE ZEST, TO GARNISH**

Stir all the ingredients together in a mixing beaker with cubed ice for around 90 seconds.
Strain into a chilled coupe and garnish with a small twist of orange zest.

•

NB: You might like to add a touch of sugar syrup if you have a sweet tooth,
or depending on what Scotch you use.

Rob Roy Macgregor (Raibeart Ruadh in Gaelic, meaning 'Red Robert') was an early 18th-century outlaw and, by all accounts, the Scottish version of Robin Hood (i.e. he was handy with a sword and a bow and prone to starting fights with people who had more money than he did – which was more or less everyone.) Try as I might, I could not find any connection between this ginger-haired man (hence the 'Red' in his name) and perfectly refined mixed drinks... Until 1894 that is.

Around 150 years after Red Robert died, the story of his life was made into an operetta by the American composer Reginald De Koven. During the late 19th century, it was common for drinks to be created in honour of new musicals or plays. The trend continued into the early years of cinema, with drinks like Blood & Sand (see page 122), Greta Garbo and Mae West. This cocktail is thought to have been created at the Waldorf Hotel in New York, just around the corner from Herald Square, where the Rob Roy show first opened.

One notable difference between the Rob Roy and the Manhattan (see page 105) is that the former historically calls for orange bitters instead of the Angostura or Boker's bitters used in a Manhattan. This adds a slightly fresher note to the drink that, depending on what Scotch you use, can do a fantastic job of brightening the drink and avoiding the sticky-sweet spice bog that Manhattans are sometimes guilty of verging on.

OLD FASHIONED

**60 ML/2 FL. OZ. DAD'S HAT PENNSYLVANIA RYE WHISKEY
10 ML/⅓ FL. OZ. BROWN SUGAR SYRUP (SEE PAGE 17)
10 ML/⅓ FL. OZ. WATER
A DASH OF ANGOSTURA BITTERS
ORANGE ZEST AND/OR A MARASCHINO COCKTAIL CHERRY, TO GARNISH**

Add all of the ingredients to an old fashioned glass filled with cubed ice. Stir well for
1–2 minutes. Garnish with a twist of orange zest, or a cocktail cherry, or both.

The earliest reference to the term 'cock-tail' comes from London, in 1798, but we're left guessing as to what the drink may have comprised... A few years later, in May 1806, Harry Croswell, the editor of *The Balance and Columbian Repositor* in Hudson, New York, tells us:

Cock-tail is a stimulating liquor, composed of spirits of any kind, sugar, water, and bitters.

If you know your drinks you'll recognize straightaway that this is essentially a recipe for an Old Fashioned (where the water component is obtained through the melting of the ice). That's because, at the time, the drink we know as an Old Fashioned would simply have been called a 'whiskey cock-tail', since, by definition, that's what it is. Flash forward 50 years, and

cocktails had advanced in both their abundance and complexity, with many drinks being modified with fruit juices and fancy, imported liquors. By that point, drinks like those consumed by your grandparents – like the whiskey cocktail – seemed kind of quaint and, well... old-fashioned.

Some people like to use granulated sugar in this drink for reasons of authenticity, but it can become a little frustrating trying to get it to dissolve in a cold alcoholic drink, so I opt for sugar syrup. Some bartenders insist on muddling fruit (cherry, orange... even pineapple!) in their Old Fashioned glasses. I wholly admonish this approach – it ruins the appearance and doesn't benefit the flavour.

The Old Fashioned is a perfectly simple, reassuringly strong drink, not a fruit salad. If you like fruit, eat it for breakfast.

VIEUX CARRE

35 ML/1¼ FL. OZ. WILD TURKEY STRAIGHT RYE WHISKEY
15 ML/½ FL. OZ. VSOP COGNAC
25 ML/¾ FL. OZ. CINZANO ROSSO VERMOUTH
5 ML/1 TSP BENEDICTINE D.O.M LIQUEUR
1 DASH OF PEYCHAUD'S BITTERS
1 DASH OF ANGOSTURA BITTERS
LEMON ZEST, TO GARNISH

Add all the ingredients to a mixing beaker and stir over cubed ice for 1 minute. Strain into a rocks glass filled with cubed ice. Garnish with a twist of lemon zest.

Contrary to the name, the oldest buildings in New Orleans' 'French Quarter' were in fact built during the Spanish occupation (1762–1802). But fires between 1788 and 1794 destroyed the 'first generation' French Creole properties, so the majority of the buildings we see today were raised during the early part of the 19th century after the US had taken possession. At that time, Mississippi steamboats facilitated excellent trade routes with more northerly states and the Gulf of Mexico offered a gateway to transatlantic trading, making New Orleans the largest port in the south. The city grew at a staggering rate through the 19th century, with the population skyrocketing from 17,000 to 170,000 in the space of 50 years. With it came extraordinary wealth, which created a need for fancy hotels and decadent bars.

One such hotel was The Commercial, which was founded by Antonio Monteleone on the corner of Royal and Chartres, in 1886. This French Quarter hotel has remained in the Monteleone family ever since, having been expanded numerous times, before being mostly demolished and rebuilt into its current state in 1954. Perhaps the most notable feature of the hotel is the

Carousel Bar, which was originally built in 1949. The bar is a circular 'island' style, seats 25 guests, and rotates at a rate of one revolution every 15 minutes – slow enough so you don't get dizzy but fast enough to disorientate (especially after a few cocktails).

Speaking of cocktails, it was an earlier, non-rotating, iteration of the Carousel Bar where the Vieux Carré was first mixed. Walter Bergeron was the head bartender there during the 1930s, and following the drink's creation, the cocktail featured in the 1937 publication *Famous New Orleans Drinks and How to Mix 'em*.

In structure, the drink sits somewhere between a Manhattan (see page 105) and a Sazerac (see page 192). There are some provocative pairings of ingredients here though: rye does battle with cognac and two varieties of bitters have a face-off. In many ways it is both a Manhattan and a Sazerac in the same glass, where the absinthe has been replaced with Benedictine liqueur. That last part is a critical element to the success of the Vieux Carré, however, as it brings sweetness and harmonizes the floral, fruity cognac with the spice of the rye.

WHISKY MAC

45 ML/1½ FL. OZ. ABERFELDY 12-YEAR-OLD SCOTCH WHISKY
30 ML/1 FL. OZ. STONE'S ORIGINAL GINGER WINE

Add all the ingredients to a rocks glass filled with cubed ice and stir for 1 minute. That's it.

There exists a very small category of mixed drinks that rarely appear on cocktail menus yet they are well known to virtually anyone who has ever picked up a glass of booze. These drinks require no introduction and to make a fuss over them would be to miss the point entirely. They are the corduroy of the drinks world (never out of fashion, never in fashion): familiar and accessible, but not appreciated enough. And just like corduroy, on the rare occasions that we do choose to try them out, we find them to be an altogether agreeable fit. The Whisky Mac is one of these drinks. When was the last time you ordered one in a bar? You probably never have. But you are aware of it and you know what it tastes like – whisky and ginger.

Most recipes for a Whisky Mac state that you must use Stone's Original Ginger Wine as the ginger component of the cocktail. I doubt a Whisky Mac has ever been made with anything other than Stone's. For those of you who haven't tried Stone's Original, I can tell you that it's not quite a wine and not quite a liqueur.

It's made by fermenting a combination of overripe grapes and ginger, then fortifying it with spirit, sweetener and flavourings. Emphasis on the sweetener. At 13.9 per cent ABV it'll more likely be the sugar that gets you before the alcohol does. The flavour of Stone's is great, though, like every iteration of ginger you have ever had, from the thinly sliced stuff you get with sushi,

to candied root ginger, all the way to ginger nut biscuits. Along with the likes of Pimm's (which has a similar flavour) Stone's is one of the greatest names in dependable British aperitifs.

In a similar way to the Godfather (Scotch and amaretto) and the Rusty Nail (see page 109), the Whisky Mac is kind of like a DIY Scotch whisky liqueur. The difference here being the innately wonderful marriage of ingredients that is ginger and Scotch. I say innate, but this is of course by design. That fragrant spice of ginger plays better with Scotch than any other ingredient I can think of. The trick is to pick the right kind of Scotch.

I would avoid any amount of peat characteristic and stick to a lighter style of malt or a blended whisky. Ideally, we should be mixing with a dram that is honeyed, but also full of green characteristics and perhaps some underlying spice. This will give the ginger wine something to latch on to: a palette of flavours for it to work with.

The finished effect should not be the taste of Scotch and ginger, but the taste of an entirely new drink. A drink that you just mixed and that will never be recreated in the same way again. It's in these drinks – the ones that were simply meant to be and are better than the sum of their parts – that we can identify what a great cocktail should be.

BLOOD & SAND

35 ML/1¼ FL. OZ. DEWAR'S WHITE LABEL WHISKY
35 ML/1¼ FL. OZ. CHERRY HEERING LIQUEUR
35 ML/1¼ FL. OZ. MARTINI ROSSO VERMOUTH
35 ML/1¼ FL. OZ. FRESH ORANGE JUICE

Shake all the ingredients in a cocktail shaker with cubed ice and
strain into a chilled martini glass.

This drink was on the menu at the first cocktail bar I worked at. It was my least favourite of all the cocktails we served and I distinctly remember it reminding me of vomit. I came to love it later, however, and more than most I think this drink is a great reflection of its name. Now that I've sold it to you so well, let's discuss its origins and ingredients!

The drink was named after the 1922 Rudolf Valentino film of the same name. It's a silent movie about a bullfighter, which completely explains the blood and sand connection. Exactly who invented the drink is not known, but the first time the recipe was published, like so many other drinks, was in Harry Craddock's *The Savoy Cocktail Book* (1930).

The drink calls for equal parts Scotch, cherry brandy, sweet vermouth and orange juice, which might go some way towards explaining my initial distaste – these are not ingredients you imagine would pair nicely. Indeed, it would seem that the bartender responsible committed the cardinal sin of mixing drinks by colour rather than flavour, since the vermouth and cherry brandy are both red (blood) and the Scotch and orange juice are both orange (sand). Serendipity should never be underestimated, however – after all, Teflon, plastic and even the colour mauve were all invented by accident! The same luck was granted to the inventor of the Blood & Sand. He was presumably only looking for a nice-coloured drink, and what he ended up with was a fortuitous and flavoursome combination of ingredients. Whisky is the backbone of this cocktail, but you can also expect acidity, sweetness and big competition between all the powerful aromatics.

IRISH COFFEE

60 ML/2 FL. OZ. DOUBLE/HEAVY CREAM
150 ML/5 FL. OZ. BREWED COFFEE (I RECOMMEND SOMETHING FLORAL AND PEACHY)
35 ML/1¼ FL. OZ. GREEN SPOT IRISH WHISKEY
1 TSP SUGAR

Put the cream in a cream whipper (or beat it by hand in a stainless-steel bowl) and warm it over a second bowl filled with hot water for 30 minutes. Brew the coffee, pour it into a heatproof glass then add the sugar and whisky and allow to cool in the cup for 5–10 minutes. Dispense the warmed cream on top and serve immediately.

I have long preached that Irish coffee is one of the world's biggest abominations. Indeed, even the finest Irish whiskey and most delicious coffee can often do a very good job of obliterating each others' redeeming features, resulting in slightly alcoholic coffee with a peculiar, 'woody' taste to it.

Now that I've finished burying the entire concept of an Irish coffee, it's time to reveal the only recipe that I would ever use to combine the two in liquid harmony. To explain, first let's look at the origins of Irish coffee to understand the reason for its existence.

It's the famous wet winter of 1942 and consequent grounded planes at Shannon Airport in Ireland that force delayed passengers to hole up in the airport bar. Bartender Joe Sheridan observes his weary patrons and takes the unprecedented step, which eludes so many bartenders, of inventing a classic cocktail. Whether it was known to him or not, the combination of sugar, fat, alcohol and caffeine provides everything the body needs in situations that demand extreme levels of pick-me-up-ness.

The key to making a great Irish coffee is matching the coffee and whiskey sympathetically. To do this we must first find the character traits they have in common. This might be the caramel character shared by Redbreast 12-year-old and a single-origin coffee from Guatemala, for example. I also believe that lighter whiskies and coffees tend to work better, which is as good a reason as any to continue using Irish whiskey.

The second important consideration is temperature. Make the drink too hot and it becomes spirity and unpleasant, requiring more sugar to counteract the dryness of the alcohol. It must be balanced with the cream on top, which acts as a kind of insulation blanket for the lips as you sip through to the main event. I prefer to serve the cream and coffee at the same temperature. I would always recommend making the coffee in a cafetière/French press, which gives the greatest clarity in the cup and allows the flavour of the coffee to shine through. Also, use white sugar, not brown, which will distort the flavour of the both the coffee and the whiskey.

RUM

RUM HAS A REPUTATION AS THE
REVOLUTIONARY SPIRIT AND IS THE
ESSENTIAL ELEMENT IN THE CLASSIC CUBAN
DRINK, THE MOJITO, BUT IT IS ALSO KEY TO
PLAYFUL TIKI-STYLE MOVEMENT COCKTAILS,
FROM THE MAI TAI TO THE ZOMBIE.

CORN 'N' OIL

50 ML/1⅔ FL. OZ. AGED BARBADOS RUM
10 ML/⅓ FL. OZ. FRESH LIME JUICE
10 ML/⅓ FL. OZ. JOHN D. TAYLOR'S VELVET FALERNUM
A FEW DASHES OF ANGOSTURA BITTERS
A LIME WEDGE, TO GARNISH

Shake everything except the bitters in a cocktail shaker with cubed ice and strain
into an ice-filled tumbler. Top with the bitters and garnish with wedge of lime.

Here is a drink with a title that seems to speak of nature, and of simpler times – an honest day's toil on the farm perhaps? It reminds us that the 'a' and 'd' in 'and' are expendable after all, but more importantly it shows us that a cocktail's name can indeed be formed from ingredients that don't feature in the recipe for the drink. There is no corn, or even corn-based spirit, in a Corn 'n' Oil. No oil, either.

Corn 'n' Oil is really just a rum sour that's spiked with the sweet and limey spiced liqueur called falernum. The earliest reference to falernum that I could find comes from the literary magazine *All the Year Round*, which was owned and edited by Charles Dickens, Jr. In a copy from 1892, an unnamed author described the drink as 'a curious liqueur composed from rum and lime juice.' Another reference to the liqueur crops up in an article entitled 'Falernum' that appeared in *The Philadelphia Inquirer* on 2 August 1896. This time we're treated to an actual recipe, which basically conforms to classic punch ratios (though it switches the ratio of sour and sweet, making for a kind of punch-liqueur):

1 PART LIME JUICE, 2 PARTS SUGAR SYRUP, 3 PARTS RUM, 4 PARTS WATER

Add almonds (almond extract) and allow the mixture to rest for a week. After resting bottle and serve over cracked ice with a teaspoon of wormwood bitters or substitute good quality bitters.

During my research of the history of the Corn 'n' Oil cocktail, the more I read, the more it struck me that this drink is in fact a recipe for falernum – a recipe for falernum that, paradoxically, *contains* falernum. Which rather begs the question – where the hell did the name Corn 'n' Oil come from? Well, most bartenders agree that the oil part of the name comes from the practice of floating black rum or bitters on top of the drink to simulate an oil spill. But nobody has a clue where the 'corn' part came from, so it doesn't tend to get mentioned. Nobody *had* a clue, I should say…

Barbados, like most of the Caribbean colonies, had become devoutly religious by the 19th century. This was partly thanks to frequent visits from European missionaries, and partly because the brutality of colonial life unequivocally proved the existence of the Devil, so surely there had to be a God too, right? Falernum liqueur may have gotten its name via one of these missionaries or some other, equally learned individual, as it sounds suspiciously close to the legendary Falernian wine that was produced on the slopes of Mount Falernus during the time of Jesus.

I tell you this because an ecclesiastical naming policy may have crept into the christening of the Corn 'n' Oil cocktail too. An extensive snoop around The Bible uncovers this passage from Deuteronomy: 'That I will give you the rain of your land in His due season, the first rain and the latter rain, that thou mayest gather in thy corn, and thy wine, and thine oil.'

Whether you take the 'wine' part to mean the rum or the falernum, all that is required to complete God's trio of flavours is the corn and the oil. So there you have it: Corn 'n' Oil – alchoholic manna from heaven.

CUBA LIBRE

HALF A LIME
50 ML/1⅔ FL. OZ. AGED WHITE RUM
120 ML/4 FL. OZ. CHILLED COCA-COLA

In accordance with the version of this drink in Charles H. Baker's *Gentleman's Companion* (1939),
I'm a strong advocate of a quick lime muddle as the first step of construction. Squeeze the
lime juice into a separate vessel, and drop the spent shell into a highball glass.
Squash it to remove the oils, then add cubed ice, rum, lime juice and cola.
Give it a good stir with a barspoon and add more ice or cola if desired.

More often than not the simplest drinks are the best. This is certainly true of the Cuba Libre, which comprises only two ingredients plus a very necessary garnish. Some would argue this isn't a cocktail at all, but a spirit and mixer. But those folks fail to recognize the genius of Coca-Cola as a bittersweet ingredient and the complexity of its composition. A quick scan over the key flavours of Coca-Cola – lemon, orange, lime, cinnamon, nutmeg, lavender, coriander and neroli, shows a set of ingredients that have coupled historically with rum in punches and other cocktails. What this means is that the affinity between rum and cola is a favourable accident.

The Cuba Libre ('Free Cuba') is named of course for the Cuban War of Independence (1895–98). We can be sure that this drink didn't exist in Cuba prior to this, because Coca-Cola wasn't available there until after the war, and not bottled for export until 1899. The year of the birth of the Cuba Libre cocktail is cited as 1900, and in an unprecedented turn of events, this was sworn under a legal affidavit by a man named Fausto Rodriguez in 1960. Rodriguez was a messenger with the US Army Signal Corps who claimed to have walked into a Havana bar in 1900 and bore witness to an officer by the name of Captain Russell, ordering a Bacardi and Coca-Cola on ice with a wedge of lime. More soldiers arrived and a second round was ordered, to which the bartenders suggested a toast of ¡Por Cuba Libre! It later transpired that Rodriguez was on the Bacardi payroll and that the affidavit only came to light as a result of

a full-age advertisement in Life magazine taken out by Bacardi in 1966. I suspect the bar story has some truth to it. But as for the brand, well, that's anyone's guess.

Whatever the origins, the drink travelled north to the US and quickly became popular in the southern states. By 1920 there were 1,000 Coca-Cola bottling plants and rum was the go-to adulterator. This practice was sustained during Prohibition, as Caribbean rum was one of the few spirits that found its way across the US border. The Cuba Libre became the most dependable beverage, especially with wartime rationing. During World War II, cola was distributed among soldiers, so there was a good supply to mix with the influx of rum.

The drink's celebrity status was however confirmed in 1945 with the hit song 'Rum and Coca-Cola' by the Minnesotan trio, the Andrews Sisters. The melody had been previously published as the work of Trinidadian composer Lionel Belasco on a song titled 'L'Année Passée', which was in turn based on a folk song from Martinique. The lyrics to 'Rum and Coca-Cola' were provided by Rupert Grant, a calypso musician from Trinidad (stage name Lord Invader), and he adjusted the song to reference the off-duty activities of American soldiers. The song was a huge hit among the locals, despite the sisters faux-Caribbean accents, the allusion to prostitution, the glorification of drinking and free advertising for Coca-Cola. Perhaps it was the transformative nature of the song, with its weird lyrics and kooky accents. Maybe it was just the fact that rum and cola is a fantastic drink.

DAIQUIRI

60 ML/2 FL. OZ. BACARDI CARTA BLANCA RUM
15 ML/½ FL. OZ. FRESH LIME JUICE
10 ML/2 TSP SUGAR SYRUP (SEE PAGE 17)

Add all the ingredients to a cocktail shaker and shake vigorously with cubed ice for at least 30 seconds. Strain into a frozen coupe. Don't garnish it – there's no point – the drink will be gone before you even notice it's there.

During the course of the Spanish-American War in 1898, thousands of acres of Cuban sugar plantations passed into American ownership. US control over mining also expanded, and this resulted in a huge influx of expatriated American workers to Cuba in the latter years of the 19th century. Jennings Cox was one such man, an American mining engineer who in 1896 worked for the Spanish-American Iron Company, near the village of Daiquirí, close to Santiago de Cuba. Conditions in the Sierra Maestra region of Cuba was tough (yellow fever was highly prevalent) and the workers were compensated (in part) with tobacco and Bacardi Carta Blanca rum rations.

The story goes that Cox was entertaining some friends with cocktails one evening when he ran out of gin. Not wishing to end the party early, he called upon a bottle of Bacardi rum, serving it mixed with sugar, 'lemons' and water, and pouring it into a tall glass filled with ice. The recipe for this 'Daiquiri' was recorded by Mr. Cox on a handwritten sheet of paper. There are some obvious discrepancies between Cox's original formula and the standard accepted Daiquiri of today. Most notable is that the drink was served long, but with the simultaneous rise of the Martini in the early 20th century, the drink seems to have shifted allegiances to the coupe glass. Cox's version also calls for lemon juice instead of lime, but there's a little more to this than meets the eye. Limes were far more common in Cuba than lemons at that time (they still are) and were known to Cubans as limón, so it's quite likely that what Cox was really referring to was a lime after all. While the above creation story seems the most credible, there

are many others that place American military officers and even Don Facundo Bacardí Masso at the crime scene (who presumably appeared as a ghost since he died in 1886). All of this, of course, is slightly fatuous, it doesn't take a mining engineer to work out that a drink as simple as this probably pre-dates Jennings Cox, albeit under different titles. Surely many a rum punch has existed containing only rum, lime, sugar and water? And you only need to look at the Brazilian Caipirinha to see a cousin of the Daiquiri, comprising much the same ingredients all served over ice.

The Daiquiri is not a forgiving cocktail when it comes to subtle changes in its formula, and one of the things that really rattles me when it comes to the Daiquiri, is when it is confused with a Sour. Now, the sour family of cocktails are a simple bunch: four parts spirit, two parts citrus, one part sugar – you can't go wrong really. A proper Daiquiri cannot be made like this though, as the light, Cuban-style rum is easily overshadowed by all that sweet and sour. This cocktail is about discretion and finesse, and to balance it correctly, you need a higher ratio of rum: eight parts rum, one part lime, and just over one part sugar (depending on how sweet your sugar syrup is). With this formula, the drink is less opaque, and seems to glow with a soft turquoise luminance. It tastes far better too, as those soft *aguardiente* notes are gently sweetened, penetrating through fleshy citrus with grace. Also, the subtle sourness means you can skull three of them in quick succession and not experience that puffy mouth feeling that comes from one too many sweet and sour cocktails.

DARK & STORMY

120 ML/4 FL. OZ. LUSCOMBE ORGANIC HOT GINGER BEER
50 ML/1⅔ FL. OZ. GOSLINGS BLACK SEAL RUM
A LIME WEDGE

Build the drink into a highball glass filled with plenty of cubed ice. Unlike most cocktails, it's nice to take a backwards approach and add the rum to the glass last, along with a squashed wedge of lime. This means you get the full effect of the storm as the light and heavy liquids fight to remain separate.

There are only a handful of cocktails on the planet that are legally trademarked, and for reasons unknown, all but one of them (the Sazerac) is based on rum. The Dark 'n' Stormy is one such drink, made using Gosling's Black Seal rum, ginger beer and, occasionally, lime juice. It has been under the stewardship of Gosling Brothers in Bermuda since it first manifested itself around the time of World War I. The flavour pairing has more distant origins and of course you're free to call a dark rum and ginger whatever you like, but if you're using the name Dark 'n' Stormy) (or Dark & Stormy) on a cocktail menu or even in a book, you are legally obliged to use Gosling's in the recipe. This is no great hardship, as Black Seal is a benchmark blend featuring Jamaican rum and sweet-lingering Guyanese, topped off with a good slug of spirit caramel for added effect. Gosling's first trademarked the drink in the late 1970s, and since then, Bermuda has become its unofficial home. Its spiritual home is of course, at sea, which makes Bermuda as good a choice as any as it's nearly 1,000 km (620 miles) from the nearest landmass.

By the late 19th century, the spice trade on some Caribbean islands, like Grenada, had surpassed that of sugar. Merchant sailors, who plied their trade between the sticky ports of the Caribbean and the British Isles, would regularly transport shipments of rum alongside their spices. These spices appealed to blenders, who used them to flavour their rums, but they were also used to make sodas and medicinal tonics. Ginger beer was the flavour of Victorian Britain, as just like tea, it was a celebration of the Empire's conquests abroad. The British Royal Navy took a keen interest in the stuff and began provisioning it on board their ships. Perhaps it was an attempt to curb alcoholism among the ship's crew, or to help with sea sickness, or maybe it even served as a heartening taste of home – either way it was popular enough that between 1860 and 1920 the Royal Navy Dockyard on Ireland Island (in Bermuda) had its own ginger beer bottling plant. And even though there's no documented evidence to prove it, it's not too much of a stretch to suggest that some sailors experimented with mixing their rum ration with ginger beer.

Back in London, the city was awash with ginger beer, with street vendors on every corner peddling their own unique recipes. One of them, William John Barritt, travelled to Bermuda in 1874 and opened up shop in Hamilton. Even today, after five generations, Barritt's is still going strong. Gosling's themselves have dabbled in a ginger beer called 'Gosling's Stormy Ginger Beer', which is touted as 'the only ginger beer created strictly to make Dark 'n' Stormy cocktails'. It's alright stuff, but finer specimens can be found if you hunt around. My personal preference lies with the bottle-fermented kind.

As for the name of the drink, that was likely chosen on account of its brooding appearance – dark clouds of alcohol and spice engulfing each other in a disquieting fashion. But the term 'Dark and Stormy' may have been borrowed from *Paul Clifford*, a successful novel of 1830 by Edward Bulwer-Lytton. The opening paragraph begins, 'It was a dark and stormy night; the rain fell in torrents', and it is often invoked as the archetypal example of melodramatic prose in fiction writing.

EL PRESIDENTE

50 ML/1⅔ FL. OZ. AGED BLENDED RUM
35 ML/1¼ FL. OZ. DOLIN BLANC VERMOUTH DE CHAMBERY
5 ML/1 TSP PIERRE FERRAND DRY ORANGE CURACAO

Use a barspoon to stir the ingredients together in a mixing beaker over cubed ice.
Strain into a chilled coupe.

An altogether under-recognized and under-ordered cocktail, El Presidente is a lost treasure from the golden age of the Cuban Club de Cantineros. It was invented in Havana at some point during American Prohibition and probably named for Gerardo Machado – a man who would score a B+ on the Latin American dictator brutality scale – who served as president from 1925 to 1933. Many historians point to Eddie Woelke, an American bartender at the Jockey Club in Havana for the creation of both the El Presidente and the Mary Pickford cocktail (rum, pineapple, maraschino and grenadine).

The drink later became the house serve at Club El Chico in New York's Greenwich village, which was run by Spanish immigrant Benito Collada. Following prohibition, El Chico had its own brand of Cuban rum bottled for use in the drink. In 1949, *Esquire's Handbook for Hosts* commented: 'The vanguard of Manhattan cognoscenti has discovered what regulars of El Chico in the Village have known for many a moon: the El Presidente cocktail is elixir for jaded gullets.'

For many, El Presidente is rum's answer to a Manhattan or Rob Roy cocktail (whisky, vermouth and bitters) but once you get to know the drink intimately, you come to realize that it sits in a family of cocktails all of its own. There are no bitters for a start, instead we have orange curaçao and occasionally grenadine as modifiers. But the fact that both of these ingredients are quite sweet, and the fact that rum and vermouth are both prone to wander into sweetness too, means that El Presidente is a drink that's prone to differ enormously depending on who's got their hands on the barspoon.

The 1935 *La Floridita Cocktail Book* lists the drink simply as equal parts Bacardi Oro (gold), and Vermouth Chambéry, with a teaspoon of orange curaçao. It's stirred over ice and garnished with a cherry and orange zest. The important distinction here is the use of blanc vermouth de Chambéry, which is a colourless, sweet vermouth style, that's more herb-centric and less spicy than Italian rosso vermouth. It was originally commercialized by Chambéry producer Dolin, who have an Appellation d' Origine Contrôlée (AOC) designation on the style.

Later versions of the drink increased the quantity of curaçao and threw in some grenadine, which might have been an effort to combat the less sweet 'dry' vermouths that became popular in the mid-20th century.

It just so happens that the original recipe (very nearly) got it right, so assuming you can get your hands on a blanc vermouth, you needn't worry about the grenadine at all. For my tastes, I do prefer to drop the ratio of vermouth ever-so-slightly, however.

FISH HOUSE PUNCH

120 G/⅔ CUP SUGAR
400 ML/13½ FL. OZ. WATER
200 ML/6¾ FL. OZ. FRESH LEMON JUICE
400 ML/13½ FL. OZ. APPLETON ESTATE V/X RUM
200 ML/6¾ FL. OZ. HENNESSY FINE DE COGNAC
35 ML/1¼ FL. OZ. PEACH BRANDY
LEMON SLICES, TO GARNISH

This recipe makes enough for 20 servings. The day before you wish to serve it, prepare a large lump of ice by freezing water in a plastic container. To construct the cocktail, add the sugar, water and lemon juice to a punch bowl and whisk until all the sugar is dissolved Add your prepared lump of ice, followed by the rum, Cognac and peach brandy. Give everything a really good stir, add a few slices of lemon and serve in punch cups.

The success and longevity of a cocktail is sometimes down to the name its given. If that's true Fish House Punch must be a tasty drink, since it certainly hasn't relied on its name to attract drinkers over the years.

Punches pre-date 'Cock-Tails' by a good 200 years. The name probably comes from the Hindi word *panche*, which means 'five', and references the number of ingredients in a standard punch recipe. Counting on your fingers, you would normally have: a strong ingredient (spirit), a long ingredient (tea, water, juice), a sweet ingredient (sugar, liqueur), a sour ingredient (citrus) and a spiced ingredient (bitters, herbs, spices). There are a lot of historical punch recipes, some of which are attached to specific societies, cultures and [ahem] fishing clubs.

Back in 1732, a group of high-society types from Philadelphia got together and formed a club called the 'State in Schuylkill Fishing Corporation'. The clubhouse was on the bank of the Schuylkill (pronounced 'Skookul) River and they celebrated their self-proclaimed mastery of aquatic beasts by mixing up a punch. The Fish House Punch was born.

Traditionally, Fish House Punch should be served in a large punch bowl with a single, huge chunk of ice. The recipe however, is at odds with the punch bowl size, since this is quite a strong drink.

A quick note on peach brandy: this is very different from peach liqueur. Peach brandy is much drier and has actually seen a peach in its lifetime (unlike many of the peach liqueurs).

FLIP

50 ML/1⅔ FL. OZ. BACARDI 8 RUM
200 ML/6¾ FL. OZ. DARK ALE
10 G/⅓ OZ. SUGAR
10 G/⅓ OZ. MOLASSES
FRESHLY GRATED NUTMEG

Add all the ingredients to a large, heatproof tankard. Be sure to leave at least 2.5 cm/1 inch of head space in the cup to accommodate the expansion of the liquid. Heat a poker on an open fire, barbecue or gas hob/stove until glowing red hot. (Important safety note: wear goggles for protection and handle the poker with heat-resistant gloves.) Plunge the poker into the centre of the liquid, then slowly stir as the liquid froths and bubbles. The smell itself is incredible. Drink as soon as it is cool enough to do so.

The Flip is possibly the earliest significant use of rum in a mixed drink. Flips date back to the colonial taverns of mid-17th century America (as it would later be known) and formed a staple part of colonial drinking culture in the New World.

These days, the Flip is commonly made with a whole egg, but this is a later evolution of a drink that was served warm and without egg in it. So where did the egg come from? Well, the original Flip consisted of a large bowl to which rum, sugar (or molasses), ale and spices were added. The mixture would be stirred and then heated using a hot poker. The poker affects the drink in a number of ways, one of which was to add a foamy, creamy texture. Later, when hot pokers seemed a little impractical, an egg was added in its place in order to achieve the same creamy consistency.

But, as in life, there's no substitution for a hot poker in cocktail making, and it affects more than just the texture and temperature of the drink.

The Flip was popular in a time where adding hops to beer was not a common practice. Many beers were bland concoctions, occasionally flavoured with bitter ingredients, including roots, barks and wormwood. In a Flip this was not so essential, because aggressively heating a Flip mixture with a hot element has the effect of caramelizing and then burning the sugar present within the mixture, which in turn adds balance and structure to the drink. Heating it on a hob/stove would not achieve the same effect as a red-hot poker. This angry heating of the liquid also went some way towards sterilizing the drink (beer was generally more sterile than water anyway) – meaning a lesser chance of issues further down the line.

Couple that with some aromatic spices, the rich fortification of rum and a warm, silky texture that slides a healthy dose of alcohol swiftly into the bloodstream, and you have a formidable winter mixture fit for any table, old or new.

HOT BUTTERED RUM

50 ML/1⅔ FL. OZ. BACARDI 8 RUM
15 G/½ OZ. SOFT BROWN SUGAR
150 ML/5 FL. OZ. HOT WATER
1 TBSP BUTTER
FRESHLY GRATED NUTMEG

In a tall, handled glass, mix the rum, sugar and hot water until the sugar is dissolved. Add the butter on top, then grate over a little nutmeg. Commence drinking once the butter has melted – you might like to give it a stir if you don't want a mouthful of butter fat...

One of my favourite things about mixed drinks from days gone by is their use of dairy products. Milk, cream and butter form the basis of many drinks from the early modern period and colonial times, but why is this?

Well, it's certainly in part due to availability of ingredients. We take it for granted these days that yuzu juice can be delivered to your door and that the fruit market stocks eight varieties of cherries. Back in the day, however, transport and shipping networks were sketchy to say the least, plus essentials like tobacco, cotton, weapons and booze were prioritized. Moving fresh, perishable products around the world was all but impossible before the invention of fridges or freezers, so the mixologists of the day relied on what they could get hold of locally.

So let's take a look at a typical winter back bar in colonial America... Ok, we've got some rum distilled by the guy two doors down – [sniff] nasty, it'll need cutting back with some water (hot, because it's cold outside now). [Slurp] hmm, tastes a bit bland, let's add some of those dried spices that came in six months ago... [sip] better, needs some sugar to take the edge off though... [gulp] now we're making progress... Just needs a finishing touch... something to soften it... make it slip down nicely... butter! [glug].

The truth is that as a creative type with a limited larder, you're likely to experiment with any and every combination of everything you've got. Hell, if I only had five ingredients to play with and one of them was rat saliva, I'd probably give it a try! Couple that with the fact that humans are a highly adaptable species, quick to jump on the next trend and to overlook imperfections, especially when alcohol is involved, and you have a good argument for a Hot Buttered Rum.

When we think of rum, we generally think of countries like Jamaica, Barbados and Puerto Rico, but the American colonies also distilled, traded and drank a huge amount of rum. Places like New England played a large hand in perpetuating the triangular trading of human workers for rum and molasses. Indeed, many of the colonial rum brands were prized more highly than that of the inferior gut rot that the Caribbean islands churned out. Fact. By the time America had won its independence and gone through a civil war, production of rum had all but ceased. Bourbon was the US poster boy – after all, it had none of that 'Britishness' attached to it and could be made from the tons of corn grown in the Southern states.

So it's kind of cool that there's a few distillers in the US who have started making rum recently, including Prichard's in Tennessee, Railean in Texas and Montanya in Colorado.

HURRICANE

60 ML/2 FL. OZ. AGED BLENDED RUM
25 ML/¾ FL. OZ. FRESH ORANGE JUICE
15 ML/½ FL. OZ. FRESH LIME JUICE
25 ML/¾ FL. OZ. PASSIONFRUIT SYRUP (STORE-BOUGHT STUFF TENDS TO BE QUITE GOOD)
10 ML/⅓ FL. OZ. GRENADINE
A PINEAPPLE LEAF, TO GARNISH

Add all the ingredients to a cocktail shaker filled with ice. Shake for 10 seconds, then strain
into a rocks or hurricane glass, filled with cubed ice. Garnish with a pineapple leaf.

The Hurricane is probably the biggest and silliest member of the entire Tiki family of drinks. But it's an important drink, as it lends its name to glassware which goes by the same name. It's unlikely home is Pat O'Brien's Irish bar in New Orleans's French Quarter. New Orleans is probably home to more classic cocktails than any other city in the world (with the possible exception of New York and London). Present day New Orleans is a curious mixture of colonial French dining rooms, wood-panelled grand hotels, sticky-floored karaoke joints and all-night dive bars. The infamous Bourbon Street is at the centre of all this: a long and grotty strip of neon debauchery, masking the greatest bars in the history of the American cocktail. But some of these bars are greater than others. In the case of Pat O'Brien's, we have as abstract an interpretation of the Irish bar concept as you're likely to find. The bar allegedly started as a speakeasy with the not-at-all-suspect sounding name of 'Mr. O'Brien's Club Tipperary'. The password to gain entry was 'storm's brewin'. After Prohibition, Pat explored various ways to rid himself of all the low-quality rum that had been smuggled into New Orleans during the 1920s. The story goes that he mixed a few ingredients together (rum, lime, orange and passionfruit) and marketed it to sailors by serving it in a glass that was the same shape as a hurricane lamp.

The popularity of the drink grew, and with it so too did the bar. Pat O'Brien's now occupies an old colonial property just off Bourbon Street, but the merriment spills into a rear courtyard with its flaming fountains and garish green lighting. The tacky lights do little to detract your attention from the drink you are presented with however – as is so often the case with bars whose drinks become more famous than they are, it's the direst possible interpretation. A Pat O'Brien's Hurricane is like a dozen melted popsicles fortified with bad rum. It is the colour of a glacé/candied cherry, the size of a small leg and positively rammed full of sugar and artificial flavourings. Most people don't have the stamina, or the inclination, to finish one – if you have any sense of self-worth, I would implore you not to. The Hurricane is widely recognized as a strong drink, and while the New Orleans original may contain a lot of alcohol, in this instance it is completely overshadowed by fruit juice and syrups. But Pat O'Brien's has made a serious business off the back of flogging these things, both in the bar, as well as in sachets of powdered 'hurricane mix' – perfect for reliving the abomination in the comfort of your own home. O'Brien's even bottle their own rum (so you don't need to waste a decent brand in the drink). It is rare to see a bar capitalize so completely on the association of a single drink.

For my version of the Hurricane, I've kept things simple and made the drink a little shorter, so it's more like a long Daiquiri modified with passionfruit and pomegranate. The drink is traditionally prepared with a blend of aged and un-aged rums, but if you're careful about selecting the right rum in the first instance, I think you can get by just fine with only one.

MAI TAI

60 ML/1⅔ FL. OZ. AN EXTRA-AGED POT-STILL RUM
25 ML/¾ FL. OZ. FRESH LIME JUICE
10 ML/⅓ FL. OZ. PIERRE FERRAND DRY ORANGE CURACAO
10 ML/⅓ FL. OZ. ROCK CANDY SYRUP (SEE BELOW)
10 ML/⅓ FL. OZ. ORGEAT
A MINT SPRIG

You can swizzle this drink straight in the glass if you prefer, but the proper way is to shake it. Add the ingredients to a cocktail shaker along with 200 g (7 oz.) of crushed ice. Shake well, then pour the entire contents of the shaker into a large rocks glass. Use the spent lime shell to garnish the top, and add a sprig of mint to decorate. Tama'a maita'i!

While the Mai Tai is one of the great pin ups of the Tiki anthology, regrettably it is also the least tropical-tasting drink of this family of tropical-tasting drinks. No pineapple juice, no passionfruit, no grenadine and no coconut – it's enough to make an overproof rum float spontaneously extinguish! In fact, the original version of this legendary drink created by Tiki legend Trader Vic is little more than a Rum-based Margarita with the addition of almond-flavoured syrup. It's the simplicity that makes the drink such a genius concoction and second only to the Daiquiri in rum cocktail fame.

The drink was created by Vic Bergeron in 1944 at the original Soakham branch of Trader Vic's. Bergeron was making drinks for two Tahitian friends, Easham and Carrie Guild, when he combined Wray & Nephew 17 rum with 'fresh lime, orange curaçao from Holland, a dash of Rock Candy Syrup, and a dollop of French Orgeat, for its subtle almond flavour'. This was mixed with 'a generous amount of shaved ice and vigorous shaking by hand'. The story is that Carrie took a sip and according to Vic commented *'Maita'i Roa A'e'*, which means 'out of this world' or 'very good' in Tahitian.

The drink spread throughout Vic's franchised restaurants, and across the US, gobbling up supplies of Wray & Nephew 17 in the process. When stocks of the rum had been depleted, he switched to Wray & Nephew 15, until that began to dry up too. Vic took the decision to stretch out what remaining rum he had by mixing it

with Red Heart (which at the time was a Jamaican blend) and Coruba (a Black Rum from Jamaica). By the mid-1950s, Wray & Nephew had been dropped all together, and Vic had turned to a mixture of Jamaican rums combined with *rhum agricole* from Martinique.

Order a Mai Tai these days, and it's usually pot luck as to what you will receive. Some recipes call for bitters, while others use pineapple juice, and more often than not, you'll get an overproof rum float in there too. The original version is by far the best but the issue being that the legendary Wray & Nephew 17-year-old rum is no easier to come by now than it was in the 1950s... So just replace it, right? Not so easy. It was the key element that elevated the Mai Tai from the flat and flabby into the sun-drenched realms of Polynesia. There are only a handful of Wray & Nephew 17 bottles still in existence, and most of them are unopened. I have been lucky enough to taste it in its natural form (thanks Jake Burger), and what a rum it is – there are few available rums today that come even close to imitating its unique flavour profile, which means that making an authentic-tasting Mai Tai in the modern era is no mean feat.

As for the other key ingredients, rock candy syrup is made by heating two parts sugar with one part water, and allowing to reduce in a pan for five minutes. Try making it with Demerara or light muscovado sugar for a richer-tasting finished drink. Alternatively, Trader Vic's sell their own branded version of the product.

MOJITO

12 FRESH MINT LEAVES
50 ML/1⅔ FL. OZ. HAVANA CLUB 3-YEAR-OLD RUM
20 ML/⅔ FL. OZ. FRESH LIME JUICE
10 ML/⅓ FL. OZ. SUGAR SYRUP (SEE PAGE 17)
CHILLED SODA, TO TOP UP
A LIME WEDGE AND A MINT SPRIG, TO GARNISH

Take a chunky highball and throw the mint leaves in there. Gently bruise the mint leaves using a muddler. It's essential that you're gentle – if you crush the leaves you'll release bitter-tasting chlorophyll into the drink. Douse the leaves in the rum and give a good stir, then add the lime juice and sugar syrup. Throw a scoop of crushed ice in there and give the mixture a good churn with a barspoon. Pile more ice on top, give it another stir, then fill any space with soda. Stir again, add more ice (if needed) then garnish with a wedge of lime and a sprig of mint.

•

This is not an easy drink to balance. The mistake that many bartenders make, is muddling/crushing whole wedges of lime into the drink. This is a poor tactic, because limes vary dramatically in the amount of juice they offer up, and unless the sugar is balanced accordingly, you'll be landed with something that's insipidly sweet or far too sour.

There aren't many drinks that speak to rum so much as the Mojito. It's packaged Cuban mojo; the perfect antidote to the heady spice of a fine Cuba cigar. A liquid embodiment of all that is sprightly, fresh and spirited.

The earliest reference to the Mojito was in Sloppy Joe's Havana Bar, which were giving away a souvenir cocktail pamphlet in 1931 with the recipe. The pamphlet actually listed two versions of the drink: one under 'Bacardi Cocktails'; and another under 'Gordon's Gin Cocktails'. The latter, of course, uses a base of gin in place of rum, and the former is based on Bacardi, which is essentially the same drink we make today (though it won't be with Bacardi if you're drinking it in Havana). The dual versions were again offered up in the legendary El Floridita's cocktail book, published in 1939, which offered a Mojito Criollo #1 (with rum) and Mojito Criollo #2 (with gin). These twin faces of the Mojito have led some bar historians to suggest that the original cocktail was actually based on an American drink called the Southside.

The timings do indeed make this a possibility, because the earliest story to mention the Southside comes from the Southside Sportsmen's Club in Long Island, during the 1890s. Fizzes were very much on-trend back then, and through the actions of some adventurous bartender, mint leaves appeared in a Gin Fizz one day, and thus the Southside was born.

If it sounds simple, that's because it is. So simple in fact, that the mixture of lime, water, booze and mint has in fact been going on for far longer than than either the Southside or the Mojito. The earliest known example of this is really an early form of Navy Grog, which was named El Draque, after the Spanish nickname for the British privateer Francis Drake. Made from *aguardiente de caña*, lime, sugar and mint, this fiery mix would likely have been closer to a Ti Punch (see page 159) than a Mojito, but clearly cut from the same cloth. Whether Drake actually drank one of these things is questionable, since he lived in the late-16th century, a time when cane spirits were difficult to come across outside Brazil. Plus, it seems an incredible coincidence that one of the greatest explorers of his time was also the world's first mixologist. But if indeed he did have a hand to play in the drink's conception, El Draque has a fair claim to being the world's oldest cocktail.

However it was invented, the drink became very popular among the Cuban peasantry in the early 1800s, some 90 years before the Southside or the Daiquiri (see page 132) – another drink it is claimed to spawn from – were invented. It was also in the second quarter of the 19th century that El Draque turns up (as the 'Draquecito') in *El Colera en la Habana*, a story by Cuban poet/novelist Ramón de Palma.

The etymology of the Mojito is not entirely clear. It could come from the Spanish word *mojadito* (meaning 'a little wet'), or it might have evolved from a recipe for 'Mojo' – a lime- and mint-based salsa.

Blanche Z. De Baralt's *Cuban Cookery: Gastronomic Secrets of the Tropics, with an Appendix on Cuban Drinks* (1931) included a recipe for 'Rum Cocktail (Cuban Mojo)' and directions to make what is quite clearly a Mojito.

If La Floridita is the cradle of the Daiquiri, it's Old Havana's La Bodeguita Del Medio where the Mojito rests its head (Hemingway was once known to pen words to the same effect). This modest little boozer was a latecomer to the Havana bar scene when farmer Angel Martinez opened it on Calle Empedrado in 1942. The bar soon established a reputation among the locals for its unassuming style and was visited by luminaries including Hemingway and Pablo Neruda. These days it's characterized by decades' worth of handwritten messages on the walls, and the fact that the bartenders here mechanically churn out up to a dozen Mojitos a minute. If that kind of product volume doesn't flash warning signs at you, let me make it crystal clear for you: if it's a great drink you're after, La Bodeguita del Medio is better avoided.

As is the unfortunate norm with cocktails and the bars that originate them, a thriving tourism trade has done away with any suggestion of quality that may (or may not) have once existed here. Pre-packaged lime juice, mint stalks and overzealous measures of Havana Club 3-Year-Old rum are the themes that populate my own personal all-too-hazy memories of the experience.

PAINKILLER

50 ML/1⅔ FL. OZ. PUSSER'S RUM
50 ML/1⅔ FL. OZ. PRESSED PINEAPPLE JUICE
25 ML/¾ FL. OZ. CREAMED COCONUT
10 ML/⅓ FL. OZ. FRESH ORANGE JUICE
5 ML/1 TSP SUGAR SYRUP (SEE PAGE 17)
GROUND CINNAMON AND FRESHLY GRATED NUTMEG, TO DUST

Add all the ingredients to a cocktail shaker and shake with cubed ice. Next, dump the ice
and shake the cocktail again (with no ice) – this has the effect of fluffing the drink up
a bit, lightening the texture. The same can also be achieved with a handheld milk frother,
or even a blender. Pour into a highball glass and finish with a dusting of the spices.

Just like the Dark and Stormy (see page 135), the Painkiller is one of a select breed of cocktails that has been awarded a trademark. The trademark belongs to Pusser's, who will send the Feds round to your house if you even dream of using a different rum brand to make your 'killer' part of this cocktail. On paper the drink is not a world away from a Piña Colada (see page 152). But unlike the Piña Colada, it's built rather than blended, and topped off with a dusting of cinnamon and nutmeg. It's these slight deviations from the Piña Colada, along with the richness of the rum required, that transforms a leisurely ride on a pleasure boat into a perilous journey though treacherous waters.

At times, I have wondered if the inventor of the Painkiller misplaced a comma in the drink's name, because 'Pain, Killer' would be a more fitting description. Once, during a notably masochistic session of Painkiller consumption, with some Australians in a beach bar in Cane Garden Bay on the British Virgin Islands, which has for better or worse designated itself as the holy keeper of the Painkiller – I returned to my lodgings in high spirits. Little did I know that the alcohol content was considerably higher than I had expected, so high in fact that I was bedridden for the better part of the whole of the following day. That was

the 'pain' part. The 'killer' blow happened when I found myself back in the same bar the same day ordering another Painkiller.

The problem, as with all the world's most dangerous drinks, is the apparent ease at which these things slide down. It is a trait of the Tiki movement for sure, but the Painkiller is the grand master. For many people, a great cocktail is one that successfully conceals the alcohol. I wholly disagree with this; good integration of alcohol into a drink can focus flavour and lengthen finish, balance sweetness, and serve as a welcome reminder to slow down. But if we were to grade cocktails on their ability to conceal booze, the Painkiller would be up there with the best of them.

My version of this drink is shorter than the classic, taking it further away from Piña Colada territory and more into the realms of Treacle (see page 160). You will find that the subtle heat from the alcohol is a welcome addition, and that the concentrated flavour of pineapple interplays nicely with the spices.

If you prefer to make the classic version, I advise a ratio of 2:1:1:1 in favour of the pineapple juice. Whatever you do, be sure to use the best-quality pineapple juice that you can get your hands on.

PINA COLADA

25 ML/¾ FL. OZ. DON Q CRISTAL WHITE RUM
25 ML/¾ FL. OZ. BACARDI 8-YEAR-OLD RUM
50 ML/1⅔ FL. OZ. COCONUT MILK (PRESSURE-COOKED IF LIKED, SEE BELOW)
60 ML/2 FL. OZ. PRESSED PINEAPPLE JUICE
10 ML/⅓ FL. OZ. FRESH LIME JUICE
A PINCH OF SALT
A PINEAPPLE WEDGE AND A FRESH CHERRY, TO GARNISH

Add all the ingredients to a blender along with 100 g/3½ oz. of crushed ice (per serving). Blitz it for a good 30 seconds, or until it's silky smooth and lump-free. Serve immediately in a hurricane glass with a straw, and garnish with a wedge of pineapple and a fresh cherry.

If it were possible to bottle the concentrated flavour of a holiday by the beach, it would probably taste something like a Piña Colada. Little wonder that sunscreen manufacturers borrow the classic combination of pineapple and coconut to aromatize their products. Hell, the Piña Colada even looks like a holiday, and a lazy one at that – quietly content as it wallows in its cool and gloopy state, all ludicrous in its bulging proportions and ostentatious garnishing.

There are only two types of people in the world: those who love Piña Colada, and those who don't admit to loving them: they are a guilty pleasure to be enjoyed when nobody is looking and far more a dessert that just happens to contain alcohol than a mixed drink – a decent Piña Colada can slip down with surprising ease, with the rum passing by almost completely undetected. Yet, for many people the Piña Colada is *the* definitive cocktail – one that best represents the sort of glitzy vulgarity of Tom Cruise's bartending style in the 1988 film *Cocktail*. Nostalgia like that is a difficult sentiment to shatter, no matter how impractical the drink may be.

The good news is that it's laughably easy to make, and requires only three ingredients (rum, coconut milk and pineapple juice), along with ice and a blender. Of course, if you have access to a slushy machine, all the better. That's how they make them these days at Barrachina, in San Juan, Puerto Rico, where the drink

was purportedly invented. Hordes of tourists rock up to this joint every day, and the staff rapidly churn out the cocktail at the peculiarly exacting price of $7.81 (£6.30) a piece. The drink's inventor – Ramón Portas Mingot – created it at Barrachina in 1963, although that recipe also included condensed milk. Like most drinks, the claim is contested, by another Ramón as it happens: Ramón Marrero. He was allegedly working at San Juan's Caribe Hilton in 1954 when he created the drink. One thing that both gentlemen can agree on is that the inventor was called Ramón. The creation of the drink was only made possible thanks to the arrival of the Coco López brand of coconut cream, launched in Puerto Rico in 1948. The Piña Colada is now the national drink of Puerto Rico and is celebrated on National Piña Colada day, on July 10.

The classic Piña Colada formula calls for light rum, pineapple juice and cream of coconut. I suggest using a combination of light and dark rums, and cutting back on the pineapple juice slightly. For bonus points, you can 'pimp your piña' by popping the sealed can of coconut milk in a pressure cooker set to maximum temperature for an hour or so, which results in a toasted, biscuity, almost buttery, coconut milk that makes the normal stuff seem bland. Whatever you do though, don't skimp on the pineapple juice – buy the best stuff you can find and sweeten to suit your taste.

PLANTER'S PUNCH

400 ML/14 FL. OZ. BREWED DARJEELING TEA
120 G/½ CUP DEMERARA SUGAR
½ TSP SALT
150 ML/5 FL. OZ. FRESH LIME JUICE
50 ML/1⅔ FL. OZ. FRESH GRAPEFRUIT JUICE
300 ML/10 FL. OZ. AGED POT-STILL RUM

Start by brewing the tea (nice and strong) and while it cools, dissolve the sugar and salt into it. Juice your citrus fruits, strain out the pulp, and mix it with the rum. Once the tea has cooled, mix everything together, pop it in a bottle (this recipe makes 1 litre/quart), and leave in the fridge until needed – it will keep for up to 2 weeks.
Simply pour into a glass, with ice if liked, to serve.

Punches pre-date cocktails by at least 200 years and form the basis of the sour and fizz cocktail families. Some punches are quite specific in their recipes, while others are a touch more conceptual; Planter's Punch certainly falls into the latter category. It's been known as 'Jamaican Rum Punch' in Harry Craddock's 1930 publication *The Savoy Cocktail Book* and referred to as 'Creole Punch' by the British novelist Alec Waugh, and it probably started its life as a mixture of pot-still rum, citrus, sugar and water.

Nowadays it's not uncommon to find folk adding liqueurs, grenadine, orange juice or passion fruit to a Planter's Punch. On this one occasion I would advocate a *carte-blanche* approach to your punch-making. So long as you stick by the classic ratio of 'two of sour, one of sweet, three of strong (rum) and four of weak,' you pretty much can't go wrong.

You'll know if it's worked, because you'll experience an irrepressible desire to go back for a second or third glass. This is the whole point of punch – a convivial drink that would look absurd if served in a large glass, but positively tragic if offered only once and in a small quantity. Of course, the effect might not be instantaneous, as writer Patrick Chamoiseau reminds us: 'a rum punch takes a good six hours to penetrate the soul. Six hours, between the midday punch that wards off the sun's madness and the push before your evening soup, the commander of your dreams'.

In the past, punches were made with a type of sugar known as 'loaf sugar', which was named for the fact that you bought it in tall loaves that look a bit like missile warheads. The shape was on account of the earthenware moulds into which the molten sugar was poured for setting. Loaf sugar was graded for quality, with white stuff (not dissimilar to our modern-day table sugar) reserved only for the well-off. Most folks could only afford a loaf that sat somewhere in the realms of light muscovado or Demerara sugar, which was no bad thing as far as the punch bowl was concerned, because these sugars offered up flavour as well as sweetness.

As for the rum itself, this is not the occasion to shy away from flavour. Punch and rum co-existed in an age of British pot-still liquid stink. A slight 'grottiness' to your punch therefore only heightens the authenticity of the beverage.

RUM SWIZZLE

40 ML/1⅓ FL. OZ. SMITH & CROSS RUM
50 ML/1⅔ FL. OZ. FRESH PINEAPPLE JUICE
15 ML/½ FL. OZ. FRESH LIME JUICE
10 ML/⅓ FL. OZ. SIMPLE SUGAR SYRUP (SEE PAGE 17)
2 DASHES OF ANGOSTURA BITTERS
FRESH MINT AND A LIME SLICE, TO GARNISH

Add all of the ingredients to a rocks glass or highball and fill with plenty of crushed ice.
Swizzle for 10 seconds, then garnish with fresh mint and a slice of lime.

Swizzles are a family of sour-style drinks that are related to punches but are prepared with crushed ice and customarily 'swizzled' using a swizzle stick. A true swizzle stick is cut from an evergreen tree that goes by the Latin name *Quararibea turbinata*, but is known colloquially as the 'swizzlestick tree'. The lateral branches of the tree fork in clusters of five or six and at 90 degrees to the secondary branches, and once trimmed to size they form a perfectly proportioned, natural stirring tool – thanks, nature!

Swizzling has its origins in Caribbean and Central American food preparation, probably originating from the practice of stirring flasks of batter and dough with paddles, or from the traditional Mexican molinillo whisks that are used in the preparation of hot chocolate. It's unclear where the word 'swizzle' comes from, or whether the tree or the drink was the first to be named. One journalist from *The Southern Magazine* had this to say of the drink in 1894: 'Its name is probably derived from the "swizzle stick" or the name of the "swizzle stick" is derived from the "swizzle", upon which point the authorities are not clear.'

The first literary references suggest that 'swizzles' were common in the West Indies by the 1840s, which actually makes the swizzle one of the oldest families of mixed drinks there is after punches and juleps. I've heard it said (but I don't agree) that the forerunner to the swizzle was the switchel, a non-alcoholic drink comprising vinegar, water and spices, which was popular during the North American colonial period.

The 1909 book *Beverages, Past and Present: An Historical Sketch of Their Production* by Edward Randolph Emerson, informs us that a 'swizzle is composed of six parts of water to one part of rum and an aromatic flavouring'. The last part leaves the recipe rather open-ended, since an aromatic flavouring could constitute any ingredient that has an aroma. This gives swizzlers plenty of creative licence to experiment with whatever fruit or herbs they see fit, but a combination of pineapple juice and citrus seems to be the most commonly agreed upon contemporary modifier.

This is especially true if you are mixing a Bermudan Rum Swizzle. More than anywhere, the swizzle seems to have found its home in Bermuda. And yet, in spite of the tropical connotations of Bermuda, what with its shorts and its triangles, this temperate Atlantic island has neither swizzlestick trees nor a pineapple pit. Indeed, Bermuda is more like a slice of rural England (that just so happens to have been dropped 1000 km/620 miles from the nearest sensible-sized chunk of land) than a sultry paradise.

Swizzles can easily be made with a barspoon, but if you can get hold of a real swizzle stick, you'll not regret it, as their natural shape generates unparalleled turmoil between liquid and ice. The trick is to submerge the spiky end of the stick in the iced cocktail, then hold the stick between the palms of your hands. In this way, the stick rotates back and forth quickly when you rub your hands together, generating lots of froth (thanks mostly to the pineapple juice) and rapid chilling.

TI PUNCH

50 ML/1⅔ FL. OZ. BIELLE PREMIUM BLANC RUM
(ANY RHUM AGRICOLE WILL DO BUT THIS IS ONE OF MY FAVOURITES)
A SMALL LIME WEDGE
1 SCANT TSP BROWN SUGAR

Add the lime to a small rocks glass and gently squash with the back of a barspoon. Next add the rum and the sugar. Give everything a good stir until all the sugar has dissolved. If you prefer, you can make a brown sugar syrup (see page 17) and forgo all of the stirring, but the French tend to opt for granulated sugar, which draws out more of the lime oils.

The Ti Punch (pronounced *tee-pawnch*) is a drink that hails from the French islands of the West Indies, and is synonymous with the drinking of the local *rhum agricole*. This 'little punch' as it translates to is, in many ways, more than a mixed drink or a cocktail. For many, it's the final stage in the making of the rum, as if the liquid in the bottle was never intended to be served 'as-is', but to be seasoned with a squeeze of lime, carefully sweetened with a spoon of sugar, then stirred, sipped and enjoyed.

It's customary not to use ice in a Ti Punch which, when coupled with the typically high strength of *rhum agricole*, makes for a fiery little drink that's packed full of flavour. It's for this reason that folks probably decided to make them nice and compact. Some, indeed, can be laughably small – barely a mouthful. My friend Patricia, who lives in Pointe-à-Pitre, Guadeloupe, would make Ti Punches in tiny blue glasses hardly bigger than an egg cup. The drink would be consumed within a couple of minutes, and then she would return to the ritual of muddling the tiny lime slice and slowly dissolving the sugar into the rum. And it is perhaps this ritual of squashing, spooning, pouring and stirring, that makes it such an evocative drink to enjoy. Pound for

pound it's one of the most arduous drinks to put together, but much like a shot of espresso, the reward is certainly worthy it.

If you go into a bar in the French Caribbean and order a Ti Punch, more often than not they will serve you an entire bottle of rum, lime wedges, sugar and an empty glass, then invite you to mix your own. This means you can get your hands dirty and easily tweak the proportions to your own preferred levels of strength, sourness and sweetness. It also means things can quickly escalate, as half a bottle of 50% liquor vanishes in a matter of minutes. In these circumstances, the bartender will gauge how much of the bottle has gone and charge you accordingly. By that point you're happy to go along with anything.

Making a Ti Punch is as easy as it gets, and a great backup plan for when you run out of ice. The golden rule is that you must use *rhum agricole*, but as far as the other parts go it's your choice as to whether you use lemon or lime, and white sugar or brown. My preference lies with the latter in both cases.

If you prefer, you can use a vieux (aged) rum, but I think this drink is better suited to the feral aromatics of *agricole blanc*.

TREACLE

Add all the ingredients to a rocks glass with a large scoop of cubed ice.
Stir for 1 minute, then garnish with a small twist of lemon zest.

The naming of food and drink is a culinary art form in its own right, and one that is best observed in bar culture. With food, a name is seldom more than descriptive, but with cocktails, a name has the opportunity to be truly evocative. Take Treacle for example: you might have never had one before, yet the name paints a vivid picture of something that is sweet, viscous and perhaps a little fruity. And that's exactly what a Treacle is.

The drink was invented by late, great British bartending legend Dick Bradsell, who was almost single-handedly responsible for the revival of cocktail culture in London during the late 1980s. Like most of Dick's drinks, Treacle is unpretentious and easy to put together. It's based on an Old Fashioned (Bourbon, sugar and bitters, see page 117) but the whiskey is replaced with pot-still rum, and a splash of apple juice is added to pep the whole thing up.

Dick was adamant that the drink should only be made with cheap (brown) apple juice, not the expensive pressed variety. And it's true that substituting one for the other does result in an entirely different kind of cocktail; both are tasty, but the cheap juice offers a glossier texture and a closer resemblance to treacle.

As for the rum, you're going to want something dense and funky to ride that apple wave. Jamaican is the obvious choice, but Demerara works equally well if it's genuine treacle flavour that you're after. Feeling experimental? Why not blend the two together? You can also experiment with switching up the sugar in your syrup for a darker variety, or for maple syrup, or even honey.

ZOMBIE

35 ML/1¼ FL. OZ. JAMAICAN DARK RUM
35 ML/1¼ FL. OZ. BACARDI GOLD RUM
25 ML/¾. FL. OZ. DEMERARA 151 RUM
20 ML/⅔ FL. OZ. FRESH LIME JUICE
15 ML/½ FL. OZ. FALERNUM
10 ML/⅓ FL. OZ. FRESH GRAPEFRUIT JUICE
5 ML/1 TSP CINNAMON SYRUP
2 DASHES OF ANGOSTURA BITTERS
A SPLASH OF ABSINTHE
A SPLASH OF GRENADINE
HALF A PASSIONFRUIT, A PINEAPPLE LEAF AND ORANGE ZEST, TO GARNISH

You can either blend or build this drink. The blended version is much lighter on the alcohol kick and requires only a quick blitz of all the ingredients in a blender with a scoop of crushed ice and for the mixture to be poured into a tiki mug or long glass.
To make the built version, add all the ingredients, except the Demerara rum, to a tiki mug or highball glass filled with cubed ice, stir, and finish by floating the Demerara rum on top.

•

For both methods, garnish with the passionfruit, pineapple leaf and twist of orange zest.

Almost as much mystery and as many horror stories surround this drink as its undead, rag-clad namesake. The Zombie has developed quite a reputation over the years due to its titanic alcohol content, mysterious origins and the spectacular nose dive effect it can inflict on anyone crazy/heroic enough to drink one.

A true Zombie should contain around 75 ml/3 fl oz. rum as well as a further 15 ml/½ oz. overproof rum. Most bars charge a decent wedge for one of these, but many will reduce the rum to a more sensible quantity and lengthen the drink with extra fruit juice. If you're served one in a highball, don't mistake this drink for a long, diluted cocktail – it's mostly rum in that glass! And it's for this reason that Zombies are almost universally listed with a 'maximum of one per person' warning.

The Zombie is normally accredited to Ernest Raymond Beaumont Gantt aka Don Beachcomber, who purportedly invented the drink in 1934. There is no

evidence to actually back this up other than the fact that Don states in his book, 'I originated and have served this "thing" since 1934... Anyone that says otherwise is a liar!'.

A notebook dated 1937 goes some way towards qualifying the tale: it was owned by one of Beachcomber's waiters and does list a recipe for a Zombie. But as a footnote to that, a recipe for a Zombie was published in Patrick Gavin Duffy's 1934 book, *The Official Mixer's Manual*. Even though Duffy's recipe is not exactly the same, there are undoubtedly clear similarities.

Regardless of who the true inventor of the drink was, the Zombie undoubtedly played a leading role in the rise of the Tiki boom throughout the 1940s and 50s (it was famously served at the 1939 World's Fair in New York), and that was largely down to the success of Don Beachcomber's restaurant empire.

TEQUILA

LOOK BEYOND TEQUILA'S BAD-BOY
REPUTATION AND DISCOVER HOW THIS
AGAVE-BASED SPIRIT CAN BE USED NOT JUST
IN YOUR GO-TO MARGARITA, BUT IN OTHER
DELICIOUSLY REFRESHING COCKTAILS TOO,
SUCH AS THE PALOMA AND BATANGA.

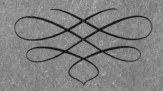

BATANGA

COARSE SEA SALT FLAKES
60 ML/2 FL. OZ. DON JULIO BLANCO TEQUILA
150 ML/5 FL. OZ. COCA-COLA
A LIME WEDGE, TO FINISH AND GARNISH

Rim a highball glass with coarse sea salt flakes. Fill the glass with ice, then add the tequila and cola. Give a good stir – preferably with a knife, as is Don Javier's preferred way – then squeeze a lime wedge on top and drop it in.

Before we get into the details of this drink – for what there is of them – please allow me to own up to something. Until I started writing this book, I had only ever drunk eight Batangas, which were all consumed on one occasion, and in one particular bar. That bar is La Capilla, in the old part of the town of Tequila, Mexico.

Indeed, tequila gets its name from this town, which in the 19th century became renowned for the quality of the agave spirits it produced. La Capilla is the town's oldest surviving bar and the name translates as 'the Chapel'. Those on a pilgrimage to this hallowed hall will have a lot to be happy about. Not because La Capilla is a beautiful space, or because the drinks are out of this world, but because La Capilla is the distilled essence of what you wish every bar could be: comfortable, friendly, and imbued with the memory of a million drinks served, a million jokes cracked and a million spirits lifted.

The minister of ceremonies and distributor of communion at La Capilla is the original owner's grandson, Don Javier Delgado Corona, who is in his nineties. Don Javier is a living legend of the bar world, partly because of the warm welcome he offers everyone, but also because he invented two of the best tequila cocktails: the Paloma and the Batanga.

Unless you live in Mexico or work in a bar, you probably haven't ever mixed tequila and coke. But it's a winning combination; the spice and vegetal characteristics of the spirit are perfectly complemented by the citrus, nutmeg and cinnamon of the Coke. This mixture is a no-brainer in Mexico, where they consume more carbonated drinks per person than any other nation (half a litre per person per day). They drink a fair amount of tequila too.

To make a true Batanga, you ideally need to get hold of Mexican Coca-Cola. In Mexico, the Coke formula differs slightly from the rest of the world, because they make it with cane sugar instead of high-fructose corn syrup and the drink has about twice as much sodium in it.

The general consensus is that Mexican Coke tastes better, but it's been proven in studies that most people actually prefer the taste of the American version. The advantage of the Mexican product is down to perception and that it's served in glass bottles instead of plastic ones. In taste tests people prefer Coke served from glass. The flavour of the Mexican variety – and this may be my brain fooling me – does seem to take on a slightly more root beer-esque character reminiscent of lavender and aniseed. It also feels fizzier and more vibrant.

MARGARITA

20 ML/⅔ FL. OZ. FRESH LIME JUICE, PLUS A WEDGE OF LIME
SEA SALT FLAKES
40 ML/1⅓ FL. OZ. CALLE 23 REPOSADO TEQUILA
20 ML/⅔ FL. OZ. DRY ORANGE CURACAO

Using the lime wedge, wet the edge of a coupe glass and then dip the rim
(exterior only) into flakes of sea salt. Shake all the liquid ingredients together with
cubed ice. Strain into the prepared glass and serve immediately.

•

Variation: For a rather excellent variation, substitute the curaçao for 10 ml/⅓ oz.
agave nectar and serve on the rocks. This is known as a Tommy's Margarita and is
widely accepted by the bartending fraternity to be, well, better than the original.

The Margarita hails from the curaçao/Sour family of drinks, and can name such cocktails as the Sidecar (see page 195) and Cosmopolitan (see page 81) as siblings. The Margarita is undoubtedly the youngest member of this socially diverse family, with virtually no mention of the drink prior to the 1970s. Having said that, Charles H. Baker refers to a tequila drink with lime as far back as 1939. The truth is that if you pick up a cocktail book published before the 1970s, it's unlikely to mention tequila at all – not surprising given that good-quality 100% agave tequila had been all but unavailable in North America and Europe until modern times.

Now, even though the Margarita is the grimy, salt-caked young tearaway of the family, she also happens to be universally better loved and an altogether more rounded, well-balanced individual. Lime and tequila have a powerful affinity and the dry orange note from the triple sec/curaçao does a great job of lifting the vegetal, earthy characteristics of a good tequila. The (optional) salt buffers the acidity of the lime, actually lessening its tongue-shrivelling effect. For this reason alone, I am of the opinion that a Margarita with sugar added requires no salt rim. That's not to say that a Margarita without sugar must have a salt rim; it's really a preference thing. If you do opt for a salt rim, use flakes and not table salt, which is far too fine and will make the drink taste like a fisherman's sock.

Margaritas can be blended, but shaking is where it's really at. The good news is that a classic 2:1:1 ratio is a fairly reliable one-size-fits-all that can be applied to virtually any tequila/ curaçao/lime combination, regardless of brand. Ultimately, what you end up with is a cocktail that charms the pants off you while you steadily slip into an inebriated state of being.

EL DIABLO

HALF A LARGE LIME
30 ML/1 FL. OZ. REPOSADO TEQUILA
15 ML/½ FL. OZ. CREME DE CASSIS
CHILLED GINGER ALE (OR GINGER BEER)
A LIME SLICE, TO GARNISH

Squeeze the half lime into the bottom of a small highball glass and drop the spent shell in there too. Add the tequila and the crème de cassis. Throw plenty of cubed ice in there and give it all a good stir. Top up nearly to the top with ginger ale (or ginger beer if you prefer) and add some more ice, followed by another quick stir.
Garnish with a slice of lime.

There isn't a rule book to correctly initiate people into the world of tequila. Most of us are introduced to it either in the form of a shot (preceded by a lick of salt and closed out with a mouthful of lemon slice) or in a Margarita. The former of these two options usually takes place with a poor-quality mixto tequila, and the latter is all-too-often 'frozen' or just badly executed (see page 169 for instruction on how to make a good one). If, however, a rule book for tequila did exist, there would be no better drink to introduce people with than El Diablo.

Granted, the name (translating to 'the Devil') doesn't fill one with confidence of the potential pitfalls of this cocktail, but in truth it's not a particularly apt name and was probably chosen more for the drink's colour and general marketability than its effects. El Diablo is a long, refreshing cocktail that plays off two of tequila's boldest tasting notes: earthy piquancy and zingy fruit.

El Diablo is genetically little more than a Moscow Mule (see page 90) or a Dark and Stormy (see page 135), where the bitters have been replaced with crème de cassis and ginger ale selected over ginger beer. And it works a treat. That juicy blackcurrant is reminiscent of the fruitiness you get in a good Sangrita (see page 174) and it softens the tequila while picking out some of its brighter qualities. Meanwhile, the ginger ale adds length, dryness and depth. El Diablo is one of those drinks that makes you salivate just thinking about it.

As far as the origins of this drink are concerned, it appears to have been invented by Trader Vic. Victor Bergeron is, of course, renowned as one of the pioneers of the tiki movement during the 1940s, which is best known for its liberal use of rum (see page xxx xxx). But Vic's drinks weren't limited to cane-based intoxicants, and the occasional tequila, whisky and gin-spiked drink appears in Vic's sizeable body of work as well as on his cocktail menus.

The El Diablo made an entrance in Vic's first book, *Trader Vic's Book of Food and Drink* (1946). At that time its full name was Mexican El Diablo, which rather suggests that an earlier version of the cocktail once existed that did not use tequila as its base. By the late 1960s, Vic had dropped the 'Mexican'; in his 1968 *Pacific Island Cookbook*, it's simply El Diablo. Then, in a rather unusual turn of events, Vic published recipes for both a Mexican El Diablo and El Diablo in his revised *Trader Vic's Bartender's Guide* of 1972. The recipes are identical; only the construction of the cocktail (when exactly to add ice and the inclusion of a straw) differ.

LA PALOMA

50 ML/1⅔ FL. OZ. OCHO REPOSADO TEQUILA
10 ML/⅓ FL. OZ. FRESH LIME JUICE
EFFERVESCENT GRAPEFRUIT SODA, TO TOP UP
A LIME WEDGE, TO GARNISH

Build the ingredients over cubed ice in a chilled highball glass. Garnish with a lime wedge.

•

Variation: You can substitute the grapefruit soda with 75 ml/2½ fl. oz. fresh grapefruit juice,
75 ml/2½ fl. oz. soda and 10 ml/⅓ fl. oz. sugar syrup (see page 17).

Paloma is Spanish for 'dove' – a lovely name for a drink – but try as I might, for a long time I struggled to find a connection between the bird and the drink. After some extensive research, I managed to track down a link between the agave plant and certain species of pigeon, including a bunch of 'paloma' varieties, whose highly corrosive droppings can wreak havoc on agave plantations. So if you've got corroded *penca* on your agave plantation (it happens), the problem is quite possibly paloma. The connection is, however, a little tenuous, and when I questioned my friend and tequila expert Tomas Estes on the subject, he told me that the word 'paloma' is sometimes crudely used to refer to the female nether-region, in Mexico. Case closed.

In most of the Western world, we drink tequila in Margaritas (see page 169) or as some kind of ritualistic shot (salt and lemon, or slammer). In Mexico, however, by far the most popular way to drink tequila – other than swigging it straight out of the bottle – is in this fine

drink. Sweetness, acidity, bitterness and salt come together in a chorus of refreshing goodness, which in the heat and humidity of a Mexican rainy season is very much called for.

Typically, the drink is made with tequila, fresh lime, effervescent grapefruit soda and salt (optional). In Mexico, the most popular brand of soda used is Squirt. There are other brands too, Jarritos and Ting being two popular ones. If you can't get hold of any of them, equal parts fresh grapefruit juice and soda, with a touch of sugar syrup, also works well too.

Sadly, the inventor of this drink remains a mystery. Some accredit it to Don Javier, proprietor of the famous La Capilla (The Chapel) in the town of Tequila. But this seems unlikely, since The Don is famed for the invention of a less popular (but just as good) drink called Batanga (see page 166), which is made using tequila, lime, cola and salt.

TEQUILA & SANGRITA

50 ML/1⅔ FL. OZ. OCHO BLANCO TEQUILA (EL PUERTOCITO), TO SERVE
440 ML/15 FL. OZ. TANGERINE OR CLEMENTINE JUICE
200 ML/6¾ FL. OZ. TOMATO JUICE
150 ML/5 FL. OZ. POMEGRANATE JUICE
100 ML/3⅓ FL. OZ. FRESH LIME JUICE
70 ML/2⅓ FL. OZ. SIMPLE SUGAR SYRUP (SEE PAGE 17)
¾ TSP SEA SALT
½ TSP GROUND BLACK PEPPER
5 ML/1 TSP TABASCO

For the Sangrita, put all the ingredients (except the tequila) into a suitable clean bottle. Shake well and refrigerate for 12 hours. Serve 50 ml/1⅔ fl. oz. of the Sangrita with 50 ml/1⅔ fl. oz. tequila in two separate chilled shot glasses.

In my humble opinion, there is no better way to enjoy tequila than with a side shot of Sangrita: earthy peppery Blanco tequila matched with intense, sweet and sour spiced fruit. It baffles me that there aren't more bars that encourage this style of drinking, since it is very easy to prepare and the result is one of those perfect harmony moments when you realize that two contrasting liquids were simply made to be together.

The word *sangrita* translates to 'little blood' (not to be confused with *sangria*, which means 'bleeding'). Historically, the Sangrita was a well-guarded secret – few people other than the Jaliciense (people who originate from the Mexican state of Jalisco) knew of Sangrita's existence, and even fewer were privy to the recipe. However, as tequila's popularity grew, so too did the efforts of the larger brands to promote Mexican culture, and that included the ritual of the Sangrita. Traditionally, it's thought that a Sangrita would be a 'leftovers' drink, comprising of the leftover juices from a spiced Mexican salsa called *pico de gallo* ('cockerel's beak' – curiously similar to 'cocktail'). Sangritas developed and commonly used fruits such as mango,

papaya, pomegranate, tangerine and cucumber. These days, tomato juice is often used to provide the deep red hue, but in the past this was achieved using only fresh chilli/chile peppers and pomegranate. Some might say that many of the Sangritas served across Europe and the US are not a true representation of the classic Mexican Sangrita. I would argue that the tequila and Sangrita ritual has got off lightly in comparison to other traditional drinking customs from around the world (Mojito and Daiquiri spring to mind).

The truth is that there is still a level of secrecy, a tap on the nose, a wink and a nudge when it comes to the Sangrita. Many bars do not serve them or have never heard of them. I put this down to the need for preparation. Ideally, it is not a drink that is prepared from scratch, on the spot. It requires the perfect balance of sweetness, acidity, fruit, and most important of all, spice. Many of the bars who do serve Sangritas will guard the recipe with their lives. It's a cocktail bar *faux pas* to ask a bartender for their Sangrita recipe, like asking a magician how he did his last trick – they won't tell you.

TEQUILA SUNRISE

40 ML/1⅓ FL. OZ. OCHO BLANCO TEQUILA
120 ML/4 FL. OZ. CHILLED, PRESSED AND FILTERED ORANGE JUICE
15 ML/½ FL. OZ. GRENADINE

Add the tequila and orange juice to a mixing glass and stir over cubed ice for 1 minute.
Strain into a chilled highball glass. Pour the grenadine over the top.

Modern speakeasies have done a good job of romanticising the Prohibition period, when the sale and supply of alcohol became illegal in the US. But it's a common misconception that illegal drinking dens in New York and Washington were filled with well-dressed patrons, sipping on perfectly concocted Martinis and Manhattans. The reality was poor-quality or counterfeit booze mixed by bartenders who were left behind after all the real talent disappeared off to Europe. Of course, outside of the US, it was still possible to get a decent drink, and there were a handful of enduring classics that were invented during this time. Most of these drinks were formulated by American bartenders working in London and Paris. But there was at least one classic cocktail created during this time in North America, just across the US/Mexico border, in Tijuana.

If you found yourself on the west coast of the States and in need of a fix during the 1920s, you might have visited Tijuana's Agua Caliente tourist complex, which consisted of a casino, hotel, golf course and racetrack, and even had its own airstrip. If you did, it's possible you'd have bumped into Charlie Chaplin, Rita Hayworth, or Laurel and Hardy. Agua Caliente's close proximity to the US border made it an attractive solution to a big problem. It's in this resort that the words 'tequila' and 'sunrise' were put together for the first time. That's not to say the drink was invented there, but a drink was invented there that went by the same name.

First appearing in writing in *Bottoms Up! Y Como!*, a drinking brochure published by Agua Caliente resort in 1933, the 'Sunrise tequila' comprised a refreshing-sounding mixture of tequila, lime, grenadine, crème de cassis and soda water – so rather more like an El Diablo (see page 170) than the Tequila Sunrise as we know it today.

While a version of the Tequila Sunrise may have enjoyed popularity during Prohibition, the drink failed to penetrate America immediately following its repeal. A 1941 advert for Caesar's Hotel (of salad fame) in Tijuana advertised a Tequila Sunrise, but the drink rarely featured on any drinks lists through the 1950s. By the 1960s the cocktail had mostly evolved into a kind of tequila sour, sweetened with grenadine, and it was only in the 1970s that orange juice began to feature. Having shed most its redeeming features, the Tequila Sunrise shot to global fame.

This widespread adoption and adulteration of the Sunrise was partly down to the growing interest in tequila in general. Tequila was the wild and racy alternative to vodka's mediocrity. Vodka drinkers wore grey flannel suits while tequila drinkers wore nothing at all. Both dangerous and delicious, tequila afforded those who dared to drink it a kind of worldly aura. The Margarita was the flag bearer for this movement, but the Tequila Sunrise led the cavalry charge.

So what does it taste like? Well, unsurprisingly, this depends on the quality of your orange juice and your tequila. I recommend using a 100 per cent agave blanco in this instance, as woody notes don't pair well with the brightness of the orange juice. Freshly pressed is the way to go with the orange, but be sure to filter out the pulp. I've found that off-the-shelf grenadine works just fine. My final tip is to ensure that the drink is as cold as humanly possible. This will take the edge off the syrup's sweetness and remove any danger of flabbiness and citrus fatigue.

BRANDY, SHERRY, WINE & AMARI

GRAPE-BASED BOOZE (IN ALL ITS GUISES)
SHOWS UP IN A VARIED SELECTION OF
DRINKS, FROM THE COCKTAIL THAT POSSIBLY
STARTED IT ALL, THE BRANDY CRUSTA AND
PROHIBITION-ERA CLASSIC THE SIDE CAR,
TO SEASONAL CROWD-PLEASERS
SANGRIA AND EGG NOG.

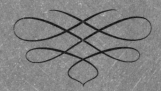

BRANDY CRUSTA

1 LEMON
CASTER/SUPERFINE SUGAR, FOR COATING THE GLASS
50 ML/1⅔ FL. OZ. HENNESSY FINE DE COGNAC
5 ML/1 TSP GRAND MARNIER
5 ML/1 TSP MARASCHINO LIQUEUR
5 ML/1 TSP SUGAR SYRUP (SEE PAGE 17)
2 DASHES OF DR. ADAM ELMEGIRAB'S BOKER'S BITTERS

First, zest the lemon. Use a sharp potato peeler and start at one end, winding down
to the other end in a spiral fashion.

•

Take your zested lemon and cut it in half. Save one half for its juice (see below) and
use the other half of the lemon to wet the rim of a small wine glass, Once
moistened, 'crust' the rim by dipping it in a saucer of fine sugar, making every effort
to avoid getting it on the inside of the glass.

•

Put all the liquid ingredients in a mixing beaker, add 5 ml/1 tsp of the lemon juice and
stir with cubed ice for 40 seconds. Strain into the prepared glass and spiral
the lemon zest up the inside.

Quite simply, the Crusta represents the pinnacle of
19th-century bartending. It's 1840 in New Orleans and
'Cock-Tails', as they were known, have been around for
some 40 years. At the time they consisted of any spirit,
some bitters, a lump of sugar and some water, all
stirred up. That's about as exciting as it got. A man
named Joseph Santini was appointed to manage the
New Orlean's City Exchange bar and restaurant. His
first move on the Cock-Tail was to use ice instead of
water. The use of ice to dilute and chill the drink would
decrease the perception of alcohol and therefore
reduce the amount of water needed, which dilutes
flavour... People won't want lumps of ice in their drink
though, so Santini used a mixing glass and strainer to
transfer the finished drink into the glass. Crushing up
sugar is time consuming, so he turned it into a syrup
that could be poured. He also added a rim of sugar to
the glass, to add textural change and a little surprise
sweetness to the experience. And how about using
some of those new-fangled fancy European liqueurs to
facilitate a subtle tweak of the flavour of the Cognac?
He added maraschino to enhance sweet soft fruit
characteristics, and triple sec to add a dry, zesty finish.
Lovely. But now it's a bit sweet. Damn. He needed to
balance the sugar and liqueur with something... But
what? Any modern-day bartender would head for the
fruit bowl without a second thought, but when Santini
reached for a lemon he was pioneering an all-new
mixological territory. A couple of barspoons of lemon
juice would balance the sweetness and plump up the
fruitiness of the drink. To finish, he thought, we'll place
the zest of an entire lemon in the glass, just to show off.

And there you have it, the godfather of fancy drinks
invented a cocktail so fiddly that it's questionable if
anyone attempted to make it. But its genius had not
faltered by the end of 19th century, when it turned up
in books by all the big-ball bartenders of the day: Jerry
Thomas, William Schmidt and Harry Johnson, no less.

CORPSE REVIVER

30 ML/1 FL. OZ. HENNESSY FINE DE COGNAC
30 ML/1 FL. OZ. CALVADOS
30 ML/1 FL. OZ. MARTINI ROSSO VERMOUTH
A FEW DASHES OF YOUR FAVOURITE COCKTAIL BITTERS (ENTIRELY OPTIONAL)

Stir all the ingredients together in a mixing beaker with cubed ice and strain into a chilled
coupe. You can add a few dashes of your favourite bitters if you want to be cool
and break the rules.

'Corpse revivers' are thought to have once been a family of cocktails all to themselves, with references going back as far as the 1870s. Engineered to assist in the survival of the morning after the night before, many of these hangover cures have been lost to time and only a few still exist today, including #1. Whether it is a viable cure for a hangover still remains to be seen, but when made correctly, this is a pretty good option for the middle of the evening.

In stark contrast to the more popular Corpse Reviver #2 (see page 39), this drink relies on dark spirits to pack a pretty serious right hook. To put it simply, we are talking about a Cognac- and Calvados-based Manhattan (see page 105) with the bitters held back. In many books, the drink is listed as two parts Cognac to one part Calvados and one part sweet vermouth.

Fruity and potent, you'll get a long, soft fruit finish from the two brandies, spiced and sweetened ever so slightly by the vermouth. But it leaves very little space for the booze to hide, resulting in one of the strongest tasting cocktails I can think of.

Frank Meier was thought to have invented #1 at some point in the 1920s while working at The Ritz in Paris. In his *Artistry of Mixing Drinks* (1934), he lists the drink as equal parts Cognac, Calvados and sweet vermouth, shaken and strained. However, the drink also appears in Harry Craddock's *The Savoy Cocktail Book* (1930) as a stirred drink with twice the dose of Cognac. Harry states that it is: 'To be taken before 11 am, or whenever steam and energy are needed'.

Here, for my interpretation of this classic recipe, I use Meier's proportions and Craddock's technique.

EGGNOG

2 EGGS, SEPARATED
75 G/GENEROUS ⅓ CUP CASTER/SUPERFINE SUGAR
150 ML/5 FL. OZ. HENNESSY FINE DE COGNAC
100 ML/3⅓ FL. OZ. WHOLE MILK
50 ML/1⅔ FL. OZ. DOUBLE/HEAVY CREAM
FRESHLY GRATED NUTMEG, TO DUST

This recipe makes enough for 4 servings. Begin by whisking the egg whites to soft peaks
in a heatproof bowl and with an electric hand mixer, or in a stand mixer.

•

Bring half a saucepan of water up to the boil and place a stainless steel bowl on top.
(Make sure the bowl doesn't touch the water – it needs to be warmed by the steam only.)
Add the egg yolks and sugar to the bowl and give them a good whisk until the sugar is dissolved.

•

Add the Cognac and continue to whisk – it's really important that you don't allow the liquid
to boil, that is unless you like alcoholic scrambled eggs! Next, add the milk and cream and
stir everything together. Check the temperature with a thermometer or probe, it should
be around 60°C/140°F.

•

Pour the warm mixture into the egg whites, whisking as you go. Pour into heatproof cups and
freshly grate some nutmeg over the top to serve.

If it's nutritional value you seek, I urge you to look elsewhere. Eggnog will not be winning awards for its health benefits any time soon. Eggnog is, for all practical purposes, alcoholic custard, or, as I like to look at it, ice cream batter.

Eggnog has existed under various guises for at least 500 years. A very early English version, known as a posset, dates right back to the Middle Ages. It combined boiled milk with spices and ale or mead. Later, in the 16th century, recipes included the addition of eggs, and the drink would be served from a specially designed posset pot. The posset is so old, in fact, that it is one of the only mixed drinks that can lay claim to appearing in a Shakespeare play – Lady Macbeth 'drugg'd their possets' to put her husband's guards to sleep.

The etymology of eggnog is not entirely clear. One explanation is the combination of 'egg' and 'grog'.

Even though 'grog' is usually associated with seafarers and rum rations, it has also been widely used as a generic term for both rum and alcohol. Another possible reason for the name 'eggnog' originates from the small English wooden cups called 'noggins'. It's ironic that a drink that has such a strong connection with the festive period in the US quite possibly has the English to thank for both its name and recipe.

You only need to read the list of ingredients to understand why this creamy, booze-fuelled custard has become an essential winter libation. Alcohol warms the blood, sugar provides energy, eggs supply protein and the fat from the milk and cream gives the drinker the necessary 'layers' to survive the winter season. And, of course, traditionally it's served warm.

Wholesome indulgence doesn't get much better than this and it is as bad for you as it tastes good!

HARVARD

50 ML/1⅔ FL. OZ. HENNESSY FINE DE COGNAC
20 ML/⅔ FL. OZ. MARTINI ROSSO VERMOUTH
10 ML/⅓ FL. OZ. WATER
2 DASHES OF ANGOSTURA BITTERS
ORANGE ZEST OR A MARASCHINO COCKTAIL CHERRY, TO GARNISH

Add all of the ingredients to a mixing beaker and stir for 30–40 seconds.
Strain into a chilled coupe. Garnish with a piece of orange zest.

The Harvard is unquestionably the lesser known of the dark spirit, vermouth and bitters family of cocktails as it's the Manhattan (see page 105) and Rob Roy (see page 114) that sit at the head ends of that particular table). But – and I fully appreciate that this is quite a bold statement – it might just be shining star of the household.

In spite of the capability of Cognac and brandy as cocktail ingredients, their impending renaissance period appears to be on permanent hold. Great liquid credentials is one thing, but the ongoing identity crisis of Cognac, which is made and governed mostly by old men in large châteaux, and bought and consumed by young men in nightclubs, places the category in a particularly weird sort of paradox where the people Cognac is marketed at are not the people who are drinking it. For the bar enthusiast, however, there's nothing to stop us from appreciating this great liquid and mixing with it regularly. It is, after all, one of the original mixing spirits of mid-19th-century America.

The Harvard first found its name in ink in George J. Kappeler's 1895 book, *Modern American Drinks*. Kappeler's recipe called for sugar, Angostura bitters (three dashes), equal parts Italian vermouth and brandy, as well as seltzer water. That's a high proportion of vermouth to brandy, which would result in a slightly flabby cocktail, so perhaps the intention was to soften up that boisterous combination?

Naturally I have tried the drink this way and I, for one, found the slight fizz to be a bit too much of a distraction from the elegant union of grape spirit and grape wine in a glass. Granted, the drink benefits from a little extra dilution, and it's not a cocktail that needs to be served ice cold either, so I wouldn't grumble if a bartender added half a measure of water to the mixing beaker before stirring. The more traditional garnish is an orange zest but Manhattan fans can opt for a cocktail cherry, if they wish...

JACK ROSE

60 ML/2 FL. OZ. LAIRD'S APPLEJACK
15 ML/½ FL. OZ. FRESH LEMON JUICE
12.5 ML/SCANT 1 TSP GRENADINE

Shake all the ingredients in a cocktail shaker with cubed ice and strain into a chilled martini glass.

The base of this drink is applejack, otherwise known as colonial America's answer to Calvados. It's a drink made from the 'jacking' (as in 'jack-up' or 'increase') of hard cider into potent spirit. 'Jacking' is not the same as distilling, though. Instead of being heated, the boozy apple juice is frozen and then defrosted but only the first liquids that defrost (which are higher in alcoholic strength) are collected. The process is repeated a few times to get the strength up and above 40 per cent ABV. It's as basic as they come, which means a lower-strength spirit that has some associated risks, as no account is taken for the dangerous higher alcohols and ketones that are usually stripped out in pot distillation. The result, though, is some rather punchy juice, full of raw, agricultural, apple flavours, which leaves behind the gift of a headache to remember it by.

Given how primitive the production of applejack is, you'd be right to think it has a long history in North America. By the late 19th century, applejack was quickly falling out of favour in the US, supplanted by good imported brandy, home-grown whiskey, and other spirits of higher repute made using better technological standards (basically any other spirit). That's why it's surprising that the Jack Rose cocktail – applejack's only major player in the mixed drinks arena – was invented.

The drink was first mentioned in *The National Police Gazette* on 22 April 1905, under a job advertisement titled 'An Athletic Mixologist'. The ad was posted by 'Frank J. May, better known as Jack Rose, [who] is the inventor of a very popular cocktail by that name'. May was, at the time, running Gene Sullivan's Café at 187 Pavonia Avenue in New Jersey. As for the mention of 'athletic' in the title, the advert informs us that, 'May takes an active interest in sports,

and as a wrestler could give many of the professional wrestlers a warm argument'.

Shortly after, in 1908, the Jack Rose makes its first appearance in a cocktail book: *Jack's Manual on the Vintage and Production, Care and Handling of Wines and Liquors* by J. A. Grohusko. The recipe calls for '10 dashes raspberry syrup, 10 dashes lemon juice, 5 dashes orange juice, juice of half a lime, and 75% cider brandy'. Then we're instructed to: 'Fill glass with cracked ice, shake and strain, fill with fizz [sic] water and serve.' It's interesting that Grohusko's recipe calls for cider brandy rather than the more specific applejack, and that it references raspberry syrup over grenadine, which was then the darling modifier of the American bartending community. Perhaps most interesting of all is the addition of soda to the drink, directing it more towards the fizz family than the sour camp in which it resides today.

Possibly the most significant stage of the Jack Rose's otherwise mostly uneventful existence, and an occurrence that cemented its place in cocktail history, was its appearance in David A. Embury's seminal *The Fine Art of Mixing Drinks* (1948). Not only was Jack Rose included, but it was featured as one of Embury's 'Six Basic Drinks' alongside five far likelier candidates: Daiquiri, Manhattan, Martini, Side Car and the Old Fashioned. That's a serious accolade from one of the most respected cocktail authors of all time.

Embury was a master at perfecting classic cocktails, and many of the recipes he penned remain the go-to formulae even today. Or perhaps his palate was just half a century ahead of its time? The Embury Jack Rose cuts back on citrus and grenadine, allowing the applejack to shine a little brighter.

PISCO SOUR

50 ML/1⅔ FL. OZ. MACCHU PISCO
25 ML/¾ FL. OZ. FRESH LIME JUICE
12.5 ML/½ FL. OZ. SUGAR SYRUP (SEE PAGE 17)
HALF AN EGG WHITE
A FEW DASHES OF ANGOSTURA BITTERS

Shake all of the ingredients (except the bitters) in a cocktail shaker with cubed ice. Strain
the ice out of the shaker, then dry shake (with no ice) to whip more air into the foam.
Pour into a coupe or a rocks glass and finish with a few dashes of Angostura bitters.

Importing wine and spirits into the New World was a long-winded and expensive exercise, so colonies in North America began to produce genever and whisky from domestically grown cereals. In the Caribbean, where sugarcane flourished, it was rum that flowed from the stills. Meanwhile, in Pacific South America, grapes were better suited to the climate, so they made wine and pisco.

Depending of whether you're from Chile or Peru, you'll likely have a different take on which nation pisco originates from. The same will also be true of the Pisco Sour, which is the signature serve for this particular spirit. The sour family of cocktails goes right back to Jerry Thomas' *Bar-Tender's Guide* (1862) and can trace its origins back further still, to the sweet and sour punches of the 18th century.

The first reference to a cocktail that sounds like a Pisco Sour comes from *Nuevo Manual de Cocina a la Criolla* ('The New Manual of Creole Cusine'), which was published in Lima, Peru, in 1903. Written in Spanish, the book includes a recipe for a drink that is titled simply Cocktail:

'An egg white, a glass of Pisco, a teaspoon of fine sugar, and a few drops of lime as desired, this will open your appetite. Up to three glasses can be made with one egg white and a heaping teaspoon of fine sugar, adding the rest of the ingredients as needed for each glass. All this is beaten in a cocktail shaker until you've made a small punch.'

This certainly sounds like a Pisco Sour, although it is missing the all-important Angostura bitters, which are ritualistically dashed over the foamy top of the cocktail.

That next, crucial step was probably taken by Victor Morris, an expat American businessman who moved to Peru in the same year that *Nuevo Manual de Cocina a la Criolla* was printed. Morris worked for the *Cerro de Pasco* Railroad until 1915. The following year, he took quite a change in direction, opening Morris' Bar in Lima in 1916.

The bar became a popular hangout for the Peruvian upper classes (people like José Lindley, the English founder of Inca Kola) as well as English-speaking expats. Some say that Morris was the first to use Angostura bitters in the drink, while others credit Mario Bruiget, a Peruvian bartender who worked for Morris in the 1920s. Either way, the Pisco Sour is a delicious drink.

In fact, it may be the best iteration of the sour family going. There's something about the untamed, winey characteristics of pisco that works very well with lime. Where most spirits fight the acidity and become a little neutered, pisco seems to thrive off it, becoming emboldened by that silky egg-white texture.

If any further proof of its genius is required, let me tell you this: in all my years working in bars, it was the Whisky Sour that was the most called-for member of the sour family. But it was the Pisco Sour that got those in the know the most excited.

This is a cult drink.

SAZERAC

10 ML/⅓ FL. OZ. LA CLANDESTINE ABSINTHE
1 WHITE SUGAR CUBE
5 DASHES OF PEYCHAUD'S BITTERS
50 ML/1⅔ FL. OZ. HENNESSY FINE DE COGNAC
LEMON ZEST, TO GARNISH

Grab 2 old fashioned glasses. Fill one with crushed ice and add the absinthe. Stir. In the other glass, crush the sugar cube with the bitters until dissolved, then add the Cognac and some cubed ice and stir for 30 seconds.

•

Chuck away the contents of the absinthe glass, ensuring you remove all fragments of the ice. (This might seem wasteful, but the absinthe will be entirely noticeable in the final drink.) Finally, strain the mixture into the empty absinthe-washed rocks glass. Garnish with a little twist of lemon zest.

For most of my 'cocktail adolescence', I was led to believe that the Sazerac was the first cocktail. At some point it dawned on me that mixed drinks had been around a lot longer than the Sazerac, but it was only once I reached my late 'cocktail teens' that I discovered the term 'cock-tail' also pre-dates this drink by a good 50 years. Nonetheless, the Sazerac is an old drink and the story goes something like this...

It's the 1850s in New Orleans and an agent named Sewell E. Taylor begins importing Cognac to New Orleans, Louisiana. The brand is *Sazerac de Forge et Fils*. Coincidentally, or not, at around the same time, the Sazerac House bar opens in New Orleans, and they begin selling the Sazerac cocktail. The drink contained *Sazerac de Forge et Fils* Cognac and absinthe, which at that time, across the Atlantic, was doing a great job of increasing France's artistic creativity and alcoholism (much to its eventual demise).

The drink was also rumoured to use bitters produced at a local pharmacy that was owned by a druggist called Antoine Peychaud. Today Peychaud's bitter's remain an essential requirement for any great Sazerac. In fact, the brand probably only survives today as a result of the Sazerac, since it is called for in only a handful of other cocktails.

There is some historical reference to suggest that Peychaud served his own version of the drink from a French egg cup called a 'coquitier'. It's this egg cup that has led some people to believe that the word 'cock-tail' was originally derived from Peychaud's Sazerac. It might seem strange that a drugstore would sell you a (strong) alcoholic drink, but remember that this was the era in which medicine became a recreational thing of beauty and the line between health and well-being was very much blurred.

Despite the Sazerac being invented in the mid 19th century, its first appearance in a cocktail book wasn't until William 'Cocktail' Boothby's *The World's Drinks and How to Mix Them* (1908). The recipe was apparently given to Boothby by Thomas Handy, a later proprietor of the Sazerac House in New Orleans. Interestingly, the directions listed it with 'good whisky' instead of Cognac. This omission of Cognac is almost certainly due to the outbreak of the phylloxera bug in the late 19th century, which caused nothing short of a complete collapse of the French wine industry. Wine and Cognac became largely unavailable, so Boothby replaced the Cognac with whisky in his book.

Ironically, a brand of rye whiskey now exists called, you guessed it, 'Sazerac'.

SIDECAR

40 ML/1⅓ FL. OZ. HENNESSY FINE DE COGNAC
20 ML/⅔ FL. OZ. COINTREAU
20 ML/⅔ FL. OZ. FRESH LEMON JUICE

Shake all the ingredients together with cubed ice, then fine strain into a chilled coupe. That's it!

The Sidecar is surely one of the most iconic yet under-ordered cocktails around. It is pretty much the only half-decent drink to come out of the 1920s Prohibition period, an era in which American bartenders were forced to ply their trade across Europe. This cocktail opitimizes a time in Europe when drinks were made to be savoured, glasses were designed to be sipped and men and women alike ordered expertly prepared cocktails that got straight to the point. Brandy and orange liqueur could easily fool you into thinking that this is an after-dinner drink, but the citrus freshens the ensemble, focusing high notes from both the Cognac and the liqueur. This is a man's aperitif.

Despite the exact origins of the Sidecar still being in question, the drink was unquestionably made famous by Harry MacElhone, one of a number of different Harrys who contributed towards making 'Harry' the first and foremost name in historical bartending. When MacElhone published *Harry's ABC of Mixing Cocktails* (1922) while working at The Ritz, he listed the Sidecar as equal parts Cognac, triple sec and lemon juice. Shortly after, he opened Harry's New York Bar in Paris. The bar still stands today; always busy, it reminds me of an American sport's bar installed in an old English tavern. The drinks are pricey, but it ticks all the boxes for nostalgia.

One of the etymological theories for the Sidecar comes from the story of an American army captain during World War I. After being chauffeured around by motorcycle sidecar between his base and (presumably) the bar, he required a drink that whetted his appetite for food while simultaneously warming his bones; a Sidecar would be a great fit.

Both Harry MacElhone and Robert Vermeire, who also printed an early version of the drink in *Cocktails and How to Mix Them* (1922), direct the bartender to use equal parts of Cognac, triple sec and lemon. I personally think that this creates a very dry and rather 'flabby' juice-driven cocktail that really isn't suited to modern tastes. Harry Craddock's *Savoy Cocktail Book* (1930) version has stood the test of time, using two parts of Cognac to one part of lemon and one part of triple sec. The balance of this drink seems to be much better, so that is the recipe I have listed here.

It's worth noting that this cocktail is often served with a sugared rim. This was a trend that reared its less-than-beautiful head in the 1930s. To this day, it's still questionable whether the sugar rim is necessary or not, and for me it simply blurs the line between the Sidecar and the Brandy Crusta (see page 180).

AMERICANO

25 ML/¾ FL. OZ. CAMPARI
25 ML/¾ FL. OZ. COCCHI VERMOUTH DI TORINO
75 ML–100 ML/2½–3½ FL. OZ. CHILLED SODA WATER
AN ORANGE WEDGE, TO GARNISH

Add the Campari and vermouth to a chilled highball filled with cubed ice. Stir well
for 1 minute then top up with the chilled soda as desired and stir again briefly.
Garnish with a wedge of orange.

The richness and diversity of Italian food and drink culture can in part be attributed to the fact that, up until the 1860s, Italy was an assemblage of warring states. Every region had its own cuisine and drinking rituals, and the manufacture of products was extremely small-scale artisanal in nature. This began to change after the formation of the kingdom of Italy in 1861, when production ramped up and newly commercialised products became available across the land.

One such item was vermouth. For around 100 years production had centred around the town of Turin, the capital of the former kingdom of Savoy. This fortified, bitter and herbaceous wine had arrived from Germany in the middle of the 18th century, where it was known as *Wermut* (after wormwood, the bitter herb that seasons the drink). As the north of Italy industrialised rapidly, Italian vermouth hit US shores only a few years after Italian unification. Brands such as Martini Sola & Cia, Carpano and Cora leveraged the romance of Italian culture to the American market, and the drink quickly became the darling of the new cocktail revolution. Mixed only with bitters, it featured on the menu at Delmonico's restaurant in New York as the Vermouth Cocktail in 1868. But as time went by, it would be as a supporting role that vermouth would leave its lasting mark in American cocktail history.

Meanwhile, Italian booze makers got wind of these so-called cocktails and thought they might have a go. The vermouth part wasn't a problem, so now to just find some bitters. Well, it turns out that pharmacists and monks had been making amaro (Italian for 'bitter')

intended for medicinal purposes for centuries, but it was only in the industrial era that the world saw the arrival of familiar brand names like Averna, Campari, Fernet-Branca and Ramazzotti. Unlike American bitters, which were effectively a 'seasoning', Italian bitters were drinks in their own right that tended to be less bitter and a lot sweeter. Pairing bitter-tasting amaro with Italian vermouth to create an American-style cocktail wouldn't have taken a great deal of imagination. And thus, the Americano was born.

The earliest examples of the Americano came in bottle form, manufactured by industrious vermouth and amaro producers, who even went as far as to place American flags on their labels. Later, in the early 20th century, customisation of this basic formula ensued as folk became particular about which vermouth or amaro filled their glass, and whether ice or soda was added to the mix. All this experimental mixology culminated in the invention of the Negroni in 1919 (see page 63), where gin jostled its way into the mixture.

It's better to view the Americano as a concept rather than a rigid formula. Contemporary recipes see equal parts Italian vermouth and amaro served long, with ice and soda water. And when you look at the primary function of today's Americano – an aperitif – this makes perfect sense. Vermouth and amaro are too sweet for pre-dinner drinking, but chilling, diluting and carbonating them tackles the sweetness head-on. Thankfully the bitterness of the amaro is tenacious enough to survive some watering down and after it all what you're left with is something, well… perfect.

CHAMPAGNE COCKTAIL

2 DASHES OF PEYCHAUD'S BITTERS
1 SMALL BROWN SUGAR LUMP
120 ML/4 FL. OZ. CHILLED CHAMPAGNE
LEMON ZEST, TO FINISH

Dash the bitters onto the sugar cube, then drop the cube into a chilled Champagne flute. Carefully pour the Champagne down the inside edge of the flute, being careful not to pour too fast, so as to avoid frothing. Pour right to the top, then finish with a twist of a piece of lemon zest over the top just to spritz the oils (which you can then discard).

According to the definition from the newspaper *The Balance and Columbian Repository* (1806), a cocktail is 'spirits of any kind, sugar, water, and bitters'. So if you mix bourbon with sugar, water and bitters, you have a Whiskey Cocktail. If you mix brandy with sugar, water and bitters… Ok, you get it. But what about if you mix Champagne with sugar, water and bitters? Well, then you have a slightly sweet, slightly bitter, and very much overly diluted glass of Champagne. But if we treat the Champagne as a mixture of spirit and water (which is exactly what it is, if you think about it), then we need only add bitters and sugar for a delicious Champagne Cocktail. The first written reference to the drink comes from Robert Tomes' 1855 book about Panama, which detailed such matters as the economy, culture and drinking establishments of the central American isthmus during the construction of the Panama Railway.

Tomes wrote, 'I profess the belief that drinking Champagne cock-tails [sic] before breakfast, and smoking forty cigars daily, to be an immoderate enjoyment of the good things of this world.'

I think most doctors would agree. Tomes goes on to recount how the drink is constructed using 'sparkling "Mumm"… a dropping of bitters… pounded crystal ice, pattered in to tumblers…[and] sugar'.

Two things about Tomes's instructions are interesting. The first is that the drink is served over crushed ice in a tumbler. The use of ice places the drink that little bit closer to being a true cocktail, seeing as water is a cocktail ingredient, and it means the drink would

probably be colder than the modern version, but hey, they were in Panama, for pity's sake. The second interesting thing is that no brandy or Cognac is called for in the recipe, as is customary these days. In turns out that most classic cocktail books agree that brandy has no place here, whether it's *Jerry Thomas' Bar-Tender's Guide* (1862) or Harry Craddock's *The Savoy Cocktail Book* (1930). The first book to include brandy in the Champagne Cocktail, as far as I can tell, is W. J. Tarling's *Café Royal Cocktail Book* (1937), where the instruction is to use 'a dash of brandy as required'.

A modern recipe generally calls for 25 ml/1 fl. oz. of Cognac to be topped up with Champagne. That means the alcohol content of the average Champagne Cocktail has doubled from about 8% ABV in the 1850s (accounting for dilution from the ice) to 16% today. But for patrons happy to splash at least £15/$21 on a drink, it's not the strength of the Champagne Cocktail that gets them anxious, but the sweetness. That sugar cube fizzing away is like a time bomb to the Champagne connoisseur, who craves dryness from the drink. But the sugar will not actually contribute much in the way of detectable sweetness, as its main purpose is to create bubbles. The rough surface of a sugar cube couldn't be better designed for bubble manufacture. and the CO_2 in the Champagne positively gushes out of the drink as thousands of bubbles form to make fantastic visual theatre. But the freezing Champagne is pretty bad at dissolving the hard sugar, so it tends to only be the last few sips that contain any sweetness.

SANGRIA

750-ML/25-FL. OZ. TEMPRANILLO WINE (1 BOTTLE)
100 ML/3⅓ FL. OZ. RASPBERRY GIN
150 ML/5 FL. OZ. FRESH LEMON JUICE
75 ML/2½ FL. OZ. SUGAR SYRUP (SEE PAGE 17)
CITRUS FRUIT SLICES, TO GARNISH

Add all of the ingredients to a large pitcher and stir with plenty of cubed ice.
Garnish with slices of citrus fruit and serve. This recipe will make around 6 servings.

Sangria is one of those drinks that only works in the right time and place. The kind of drink you wouldn't dream of ordering unless you're sitting on the beach in Spain. Lots of drinks evoke a sense of place regardless of where you are when you choose to enjoy them. Other drinks really do require you to be *in that place* to appreciate them properly. Sangria falls into the latter camp. It is the liquid embodiment of hazy afternoons, seasoned with salty morsels of tapas and the nagging feeling that wine will never taste this good ever again.

Sangria is basically a type of punch made from a base of red wine and brandy or rum. You find many drinks like this outside of the Iberian peninsular, but you'd be incorrect in thinking it has always been this way. Wine punches have been enjoyed in Europe since the 17th century and have their roots in the Hippocratic wines (or *hippocras*) that emerged out of Dark Ages Europe in the 15th century, around the same time as aqua vitae first arrived.

It was a simple trick: you take poor-quality wine and add to it herbs, spices, fruits, sugar, or just more booze, and what you're left with tastes better than what you started with, and it gets you drunk quicker (an essential feature of any 15th-century beverage). While some took to doctoring low-quality plonk in efforts to emulate the wines of the great chateaux of France (see pamphlets on the subject, such as *A New and Easie Way to Make Twenty-Three Sorts of Wine, Equal to That of France* from 1701 and John Yarworth's *New Treatise on Artificial Wines* from 1690), others dedicated their time to creating elaborate punches with wine at the heart.

The wines in question were varied, from port to Riesling and everything in between. Punch Royal consisted of Rhenish wine with lemon juice, ginger, cinnamon, nutmeg, brandy, musk and ambergris (a deeply aromatic, waxy substance produced in the digestive system of a sperm whale, no less). Ruby Punch, which appears in *Oxford Nightcaps* (1827) was a combination of port, lemon juice, rum and tea.

Of course if you live in Spain, you've little use for warming winter spices, so they get substituted for more fruit and perhaps some fresh herbs, and what you're left with is Sangria. There's no known date for the invention of Sangria (the name is thought to come from the Spanish word 'sangue', meaning 'blood'), and it seems likely that it simply evolved organically from the wider European trend of wine punches. One day it wasn't there, the next day it was, and nobody seemed to notice anything had changed.

And because we have no inventor to credit, there's no *de facto* recipe for Sangria. Red wine is a must, then there's citrus juice, some sugar, some brandy (or other spirit), then add whatever other fruits and herbs fit your personal preferences.

In my recipe I like to amplify the red-fruit flavours of Spanish Tempranillo wine (the grape used to make Rioja) by fortifying it with a raspberry-infused gin. I then use purely lemon juice (no orange), along with sugar and ice. You can easily infuse fresh raspberries into a bottle of gin (leave in a warm place for a week) or buy one of the many brands now producing raspberry 'pink' gin.

SHERRY COBBLER

60 ML/2 FL. OZ. DRY OLOROSO SHERRY
15 ML/½ FL. OZ. SUGAR SYRUP (SEE PAGE 17)
15 ML/½ FL. OZ. FRESH GRAPEFRUIT JUICE (YOU CAN USE APPLE, ORANGE OR PINEAPPLE IF YOU PREFER)
6 FRESH RASPBERRIES OR BLACKBERRIES
A MINT SPRIG, TO GARNISH

Fill a tumbler or rocks glass with crushed ice and add all of the ingredients. Give it a good stir with
a barspoon and top up with more crushed ice. Garnish with a sprig of fresh mint
and serve with a straw.

Cobblers are an old family of cocktails from the Iron Age of American bartending and were originally made from a base of wine mixed with fruit, sugar and some citrus. A sort of single-serve punch, if you will. Any wine will do, but sherry is king here – good oloroso turns into pure addiction when paired with fresh fruit, ice and little sweetness.

Now, if it were only this drink's deliciousness that made it special, I would probably rest my case right here. But there's a lot more to the history and influence of the cobbler than appears at first glance. The first cobblers came about in America in the early 19th century, some time between 1810 and 1830, roughly coinciding with the invention of the Mint Julep, of which it is a close relation. In fact, the first written reference to the cobbler was in 1838, the same year that the first Mint Julep was served at the Kentucky Derby. Just like the julep, cobblers are traditionally made with crushed ice. This approach gets things cold nice and quickly, and it means you can do away with shaking and just build in the glass if it pleases you.

Crushed ice in a cocktail presents one or two issues, however, such as when you go to tip the glass up and the ice cascades down on your face. The issue is compounded when you have fresh fruit mixed in there too, as you do with a cobbler. The Mint Julep (see page 106) got around this issue with the julep strainer, now used by many bartenders to strain stirred cocktails, and early cobblers were served in this manner too. A neater solution would, of course, have been a drinking straw.

Only problem was they hadn't been invented then. Well, that's not strictly true. The first known pictogram of alcohol consumption, which comes from ancient Sumeria, shows revellers drinking through straws shoved into a large pot of beer. During the 1800s, straws made from rye grass became popular, but they had a tendency to dissolve into mush. Metal straws and straws made from tubular pasta (yes, really) also existed, but commercially produced straws didn't arrive until the 1880s. Marvin Stone's patent for the first paper drinking straw was made from rolled-up paper coated in wax. If you were a cobbler drinker – and given that it was one of the most popular cocktails in America during the 1880s, you probably were – the drinking straw would be the greatest marvel until sliced bread was invented some 40 years later.

Some bartenders preferred to shake their cobblers, however, and that's the method that Jerry Thomas instructed in his *Bar-Tender's Guide* (1862). At that time, the cobbler was one of the only cocktails that you would have bothered to shake. Not least because the cocktail shaker didn't exist until 1872, when a patent was filed by William Harnett of Brooklyn for his 'apparatus for mixed drinks'. Harnett's shaker was painfully overengineered, though, consisting of six covered tumblers mounted on a plunger-based system. Twelve years later, Edward Hauck, also of Brooklyn, patented the three-piece shaker that we know and love today – the shaker that became widely known as the 'cobbler shaker'.

INDEX

ABOUT THE AUTHOR

Tristan Stephenson is a successful bar operator, bartender, barista, chef, some-time journalist, and bestselling author of *The Curious Bartender* series of drinks books. With Thomas Aske, he is the co-founder of London-based Fluid Movement, a globally renowned drinks consultancy firm, and as such, half the brains behind the drinks programs at some of the world's top drinking destinations. In 2009 he was ranked 3rd in the UK Barista Championships. He was awarded UK bartender of the year in 2012 and in the same year was included in London *Evening Standard's* 'Top 1000 most influential Londoners'.

Having started his career in the kitchens of various Cornish restaurants, Tristan was eventually given the task of designing cocktails and running bar operations for Jamie Oliver's Fifteen restaurant (in Cornwall) back in 2007. He went on to work for the world's biggest premium drinks company, Diageo, for two years. After co-founding Fluid Movement in 2009, Tristan opened two bars in London – Purl, his first, in 2010, and then the Worship Street Whistling Shop in 2011. Worship Street Whistling Shop was awarded *Time Out London's* 'Best New Bar' in 2011 and was placed in the 'World's Fifty Best Bars' for three consecutive years.

In 2014 Fluid Movement opened their next venue, this time outside of London. Surfside, a steak and lobster restaurant on Polzeath beach in North Cornwall, was awarded the No. 1 Position in *The Sunday Times's* 'Best alfresco dining spots in the UK 2015'. Tristan served as head chef there for the first year and continues to manage the menus. In 2016 Fluid Movement opened three more London bars, all at the same Shoreditch site – The Devil's Darling, Sack and Black Rock (the latter a bar dedicated to whiskey which won Time Out's 'UK's Best Specialist Bar' from 2017–2019. The original basement space has since expanded to include the first-floor Black Rock Tavern, styled after the izakayas of Japan, and offering a curated collection of whiskies from around the world.

Tristan's first book, *The Curious Bartender Volume I: The Artistry & Alchemy of Creating the Perfect Cocktail* was published in Autumn 2013 and shortlisted for the prestigious André Simon Award. His second book, *The Curious Bartender: An Odyssey of Malt, Bourbon & Rye Whiskies* hit the bookshelves in October 2014. In Spring 2015 he published *The Curious Barista's Guide to Coffee* (having previously harvested, processed, roasted and brewed the first cup of UK-grown coffee from the Eden Project in Cornwall, achieving international press coverage). His fourth book *The Curious Bartender's Gin Palace* (2018), was shortlisted for the André Simon Award. During the course of his research for this tome, Tristan travelled to over 150 distilleries around the world, in over 20 countries, including Scotland, Mexico, Cuba, France, Lebanon, Italy, Guatemala, Japan, the US and Spain. Next, his fifth book *The Curious Bartender's Rum Revolution* was published in 2017, taking the reader beyond rum's Caribbean heartlands to discover new distilleries in Brazil, Venezuela, Colombia and Guatemala, as well as in other unexpected corners of the world, from Australia to Japan. His eagerly anticipated sixth book, *The Curious Bartender Volume II: The New Testament of Cocktails* was published in 2018, as a follow-up to the original bestseller, and this was followed in 2019 by *The Curious Bartender's Whisky Road Trip*, a coast-to-coast tour of distilleries in the US.

Tristan's other commercial enterprises include his drinks brand Aske-Stephenson, which manufactures and sells pre-bottled cocktails in flavours as diverse as Peanut Butter & Jam Old-Fashioned and Flat White Russian. He also runs an on-line whisky subscription service – whisky-me.com – offering top-quality single-malt whiskies for home delivery. In addition, in March 2017 Tristan joined supermarket chain Lidl UK as a consultant on their highly regarded own-brand spirits range.

Tristan lives in Cornwall and is husband to Laura and father to two small children. In his limited spare time he runs, rides a Triumph motorcycle, takes photographs, designs websites, bakes bread, cooks a lot, attempts various DIY tasks beyond his level of ability and collects whisky and books.

BIBLIOGRAPHY & CREDITS

BIBLIOGRAPHY

BOOKS BY THE SAME AUTHOR:

The Curious Bartender Volume I: The Artistry & Alchemy of Creating the Perfect Cocktail (original edition 2013, updated edition 2016, small format edition 2019)

The Curious Bartender: An Odyssey of Malt, Bourbon & Rye Whiskies (2014)

The Curious Barista's Guide to Coffee (2015)

The Curious Bartender's Gin Palace (2016)

The Curious Bartender's Rum Revolution (2017)

The Curious Bartender Volume II: The New Testament of Cocktails (2018)

The Curious Bartender's Guide to Gin (2018)

The Curious Bartender's Whisky Road Trip (2019)

The Curious Bartender's Guide to Malt, Bourbon & Rye Whiskies (2020)

The Curious Bartender's Guide to Rum (2020)

OTHER COCKTAIL BOOKS:

Arthur, Stanley Clisby *Famous New Orleans Drinks and How to Mix 'em* (1937)

Beebe, Lucius *The Stork Club Bar Book* (1946)

Bergeron, Victor *Trader Vic's Book of Food and Drink* (1946) revised as *Trader Vic's Bartender's Guide* (1972)

Boothby, William (Bill) *The World's Drinks and How to Mix Them* (1908)

Bryon, O.H. *The Modern Bartenders' Guide* (1884)

Craddock, Harry *The Savoy Cocktail Book* (1930)

Daly, Tim *Daly's Bartenders' Encyclopedia* (1903)

Deacon, Mary R. *The Clover Club of Philadelphia* (1897)

Duffy, Patrick *The Official Mixer's Manual* (1934)

Embury, David A. *The Fine Art of Mixing Drinks* (1948)

Ensslin, Hugo R. *Recipes for Mixed Drinks* (1916)

Grohusko, J. A. *Jack's Manual on the Vintage and Production, Care and Handling of Wines and Liquors* (1910)

Kappeler, George J. *Modern American Drinks* (1895)

La Floridita, *La Floridita Cocktail Book* (1935)

MacElhone, Harry, *Barflies and Cocktails* (1927)

MacElhone, Harry *Harry's ABC of Mixing Cocktails* (1919)

Meier, Frank *Artistry of Mixing Drinks* (1934)

Picchi, Luca *Sulle Tracce del Conte (On the Trail of the Count)* (2002)

Saucier, Ted *Bottoms Up* (1951)

Tarling, W.J. *Café Royal Cocktail Book* (1937)

Thomas P., Jeremiah (Jerry), *How to Mix Drinks* (1862) also known as *The Bon-Vivant's Companion* or *The Bar-Tender's Guide*

Vermeire, Robert *Cocktails and How to Mix Them* (1922)

Wondrich, David *Punch* (2011)

ANY OTHER PUBLICATIONS:

Buchan, William *Domestic Medicine* 1791

Bulwer-Lytton, Edward *Paul Clifford* 1830

Chandler, Raymond *The Long Goodbye* 1953

Cook, Richard *Oxford Night Caps* 1827

Crocker, Betty *Betty Crocker's New Picture Cook Book* (1961)

De Baralt, Blanche Z. *Cuban Cookery: Gastronomic Secrets of the Tropics, with an Appendix on Cuban Drinks* (1931)

Dickens, Charles *Sketches by Boz* (1839)

Dickens, Charles *The Old Curiosity Shop* (1840–41)

Emerson, Edward Randolph *Beverages, Past and Present: An Historical Sketch of Their Production* (1909)

Fleming, Ian *Casino Royale* (1953), *Live & Let Die* (1954), *Moonraker* (1955)

Habeeb, Virginia T. *American Home All-purpose Cookbook* (1966)

Nuevo Manual de Cocina a la Criolla (The New Manual of Creole Cuisine) (1903)

Simpson, Colin *Wake Up In Europe: a Book of Travel for Australians & New Zealanders* (1959)

Tomes, Robert *Panama in 1855* (1855)

Tryon, Thomas *A New and Easie Way to Make Twenty-Three Sorts of Wine, Equal to That of France* (1701)

PICTURE CREDITS